FREE AT LAST

FREE AT LAST

Bob Moorehead

College Press Publishing Company, Joplin, Missouri

Library of Congress Catalog Card Number: 86-071102
International Standard Book Number: 0-89900-212-9

TABLE OF CONTENTS

PREFACE

A pressure-cooker world has produced an imprisoned society! Counseling offices are full of people in bondage, prisoners of their own guilt, fear, bitterness, depression, anger, lust plus many other attitudes that cripple and ultimately destroy. I don't hear much these days in the way of hope and deliverance for people who are cell-bound, stuck, if you please, by debilitating attitudes.

These "prisoners" are affected in virtually every area of their lives. The "time" they serve robs them from successful marriages, families, jobs, and even their own productivity. Sadly enough, some Spirit-filled believers, people who are unquestionably committed to Christ, find themselves at one time or another looking out through bars that lock them in and keep them from being all God intends them to be.

These chapters deal with attitudes whose prisoners God never intended us to be. Half the battle is won when you recognize the source of the enslavement. Satan wants nothing more than for believers to live defeated, disappointed, and unhappy lives. This becomes his "show and tell" program for the world to see. If the world can look at a defeated and depressed believer, one picture is worth a thousand words. The other half of the battle is won when you realize that "He that is in you is greater than he that is in the world." There is a way out. It isn't by struggle, by violence, or by strategy, but by surrender. Maybe as you read these chapters, you will discover an attitude that binds you and keeps you from daily victory. The sweetest sound in all the world to a prisoner in a real jail cell is the unlocking of the steel lock, the opening of the large barred door, and the voice of the jail-keeper when he says; "YOU'RE FREE TO GO NOW." The One who "heals all your diseases, and redeems your life from the pit" (Ps. 103:3b-4)[1] essentially said those words on Calvary's cross. Only as you hear them and appropriate them will you be truly free. "If the son makes you free, you will be free indeed" (John 8:36). Even a casual glance at the life of Jesus in the four gospels reveals that much of His ministry was in the area of deliverance. He freed people from diseases, demon possession, hunger, fear, rebellion, blindness and prejudice. What He did He does! Much of our generation is in bondage today. The world's release program hasn't worked, it's just brought more bondage. Jesus Christ alone can free us from whatever holds us captive. Indeed, Jesus stated at the outset of His ministry what He came to do:

> The Spirit of the Lord is upon me, because he has anointed me to preach good news to the poor. He has sent me *to proclaim release to the captives,* and recovering of sight to the blind, TO SET AT LIBERTY THOSE WHO ARE OPPRESSED . . ." (Luke 4:18).

Jesus has already said at the door of your heart, "You're free to go now!" In the following pages, maybe that freedom will become a reality in your life! In the words of a little chorus, your testimony can be "Thank God Almighty, I'm free at last."

Bob Moorehead

---

1. Scripture quotations are taken from the Revised Standard Version, unless otherwise noted. (Used with permission.)

1

HEALED FROM HURT

"Sticks and stones can break my bones, but words can never hurt me." We all remember saying those words as a child, even through teary eyes and choked up voices because we had been hurt so badly by cruel words.

Betty appeared to be on top of things. She forced a smile around others, but as a wife and mother of two pre-schoolers, her scars of hurt were fresh and deep. Little did her friends know the rejection by her husband, the put downs, the remarks in private, the criticisms and the coldness . . . the hurt went deep. All her life she had dreamed of being a wife . . . a mother . . . having a happy home, but the dream was shattered when she learned that Bill had had at least one affair, and maybe two. Without a close relationship to her mother, and too embarrassed to talk of her hurt with friends, she suffered in silence, knowing the day would come when Bill may not come home, and it would be all over. The hurt was deep.

Tony was young, bright, handsome, and so excited about the wedding day that was only 42 days away. He loved Celeste deeply and felt God had specially selected her just for him. He often referred to her as God's "grace-gift." She was more than he ever thought he deserved. Plans were well under way, invitations were ready to be mailed, and then it happened. A seven page letter, left at his door with the engagement ring enclosed. The letter tried to drop him with ease, but in spite of all the "logical" reasons she gave for backing out of the marriage, Tony crashed and burned. The hurt was so deep, so painful, so severe, the crying lasted for days. Hurt had claimed another victim.

Rob and Helen had 17 happy years of marriage under their belt. Their two sons excelled in sports, their common interest in snow skiing seemed to bind Rob and Helen even closer. Both taught pre-schoolers at their church. Then it came. In a routine exam for insurance purposes, the doctor discovered a large tumor on Rob's left lung. The verdict: it was inoperable. Both chemotherapy and cobalt treatment failed. From the day of the exam, they had only six short weeks to say their good-byes. Rob was gone! Helen soon became a prisoner of that hurt and became a recluse. Hurt had struck again.

Thousands are held by hurts that "seemingly" won't go away, thus, isolation sets in and people begin to die spiritually and socially.

Hurts come in all kinds of sizes and packages. They come from employers to employees, from employees to employers; they come from teacher to pupil, and from pupil to teacher; they come from wife to husband and husband to wife; from daughters, mothers, dads, brothers, sisters, best friends, pastors, from colleagues, and the list is endless.

Most people cover their hurts with facades. "Oh it's nothing, everybody gets a lemon once in a while," and the hurt is brushed aside . . . or stacked inside to brood and cut.

Standing in the delivery room witnessing the birth of my first granddaughter, I cried . . . not because she looked bad, but because I thought of all the hurt this innocent child would someday be exposed to. Somehow I wanted to give her an instant antibiotic that would shield and insulate her forever against hurts. I may protect her from smallpox, chickenpox, mumps, measles and polio, but I can't inoculate her against hurts, they will invariably come, and soon.

Like insects and weeds, hurts come in many varieties. In mentioning only a few, maybe you can identify with at least one.

The Hurt of Loneliness

Researchers have recently told us that the number of people living alone in America is increasing at a rate faster than at any other time in our nation's history. In the last few years, marketers have drastically adjusted the size of their products to target a whole new and growing market, the single person. The increasing divorce rate, the longevity of life, one spouse living much longer after the other spouse's death, and the later age that people are marrying, all combine to increase the number of single people today. More singleness often means more loneliness. But loneliness isn't confined to people who are single. To the contrary, many married couples with families suffer from loneliness and melancholy because of the increasing impersonalization of the times. Drive-up banking, drive-up fast foods, drive-up dry cleaning have all moved us a little closer to a "people-less" society in daily business. But sometimes, as those who have been hurt by loneliness can testify, loneliness has little to do with the presence or absence of people. It is an attitude of the spirit. You can be lonely in a crowd, and loneliness hurts.

The Hurt of Idleness

Jesus told a graphic parable about workers; part of that parable goes like this:

> Why do you stand here idle all day? Because no one has hired us! (Matt. 20:6b, 7a).

Because no one has hired us . . . that may well be one of the saddest statements in the Bible. Unemployment is not just an income loss, it is a cataclysmic trauma in a person's life bringing feelings of hurt and helplessness. Maybe you have recently been laid off, or terminated. You may even be middle-aged and unemployed. Nothing hurts down deep so badly when you're asked ". . . and where do you work?" and you have to respond by saying, "I'm presently unemployed." Hurt comes by idleness.

The Hurt of Rejection

If you haven't been rejected by someone at some point for some reason in life, hold on, your turn is coming!! It doesn't really matter

11

what the rejection is, it hurts! You may have an idea rejected, a request rejected, a proposal rejected, it doesn't really matter what it is, rejection is rejection. A teen is "crowded" out of the group, that's rejection. A housewife's request for more grocery money is refused, that's rejection. A father cancels or postpones an event with the children, that's rejection. You may have recently experienced the hurt rejection can bring. It is a real hurt.

The Hurt of a Handicap

No one really knows, nor can anyone describe the depth of hurt that comes by having some physical or emotional handicap. The silent suffering is very much there, and it seems like no one could ever understand. This hurt must often be borne alone because so few have been through it. Maybe you are held by the hurt of some handicap, an amputation, blindness, deafness, a birth defect, paralysis, or one of many other things. The hurt of a handicap is real . . . and often it won't go away.

The Hurt of Grief

The emptiness brought on by the loss of a loved one brings severe hurt. Only those who have walked through the valley of the shadow can really know. You may have lost a spouse. This experience is like part of you being cut right out of you. It is, indeed, major surgery, the kind that is slow healing. Even when there are no tears left to flow, the crying goes on, and the hurt is still there. Only the Lord can heal at this point, human words seem to fail. Unfortunately, many are held by the grip of grief because they refuse to be released, though the Lord offers this release. God wants us delivered from the hurt that grief brings. We need to cry, but also remember that God never intended us to wallow forever in a pool of tears.

No matter the kind of hurt, the good news is that you do not have to be held in bondage by a hurt spirit. Hurt can quickly turn into anger, revenge, bitterness or worse,—violence.

Jesus knew what hurt was all about. He understood the pain of rejection, the nightmare of close friends forsaking Him. He's been there, thus, He is able to help like no other. The good news is that

12

we don't have to hurt continuously. He is truly a friend that sticks closer than a brother, and desires to minister to your hurts and mind. It's up to us to allow that ministry to proceed. He knows, He cares, and He acts. The Psalmist said, "This I know, that God is for me" (Ps. 56:9). The Israelites were in Babylonian bondage. Oh, how that hurt. They missed Jerusalem, the Temple, their fellow Jews. Their hurt can easily be seen; it is described for us in Psalms 137; "by the waters of Babylon, there we sat down and wept when we remembered Zion. On the willows there we hung up our lyres . . . how shall we sing the Lord's song in a foreign land?" (Ps. 137:1, 2, 4).

But the fact is, they did! God delivered them from their hurts and eventually brought them back to their homeland. You don't have to be held by hurt. God specializes in deliverance from the bondage of hurt.

The Hurt of Broken Dreams

Ted and Monica dreamed of owning their own flower shop. They carefully saved, planned, skimped, and went through the rigid discipline of projecting a time chart. They figured it would take three years, then they would be eligible for a small business loan, and their dream could become a reality. They waited, they saved, and the day came. With the loan secured, they opened shop! Through a nightmare of calamities, within 60 days their dreams were shattered. Rent escalated, unexpected sickness set in, unusual problems developed with the children, and a supermarket opened nearby with a flower shop. Tearfully they locked the door of their biggest dream one last time. Broke, tired, discouraged, they were the victims of a vicious hurt—the hurt of a broken dream.

Many of us can identify with that. Some of the deepest hurts come when we've planned, prayed and ventured in faith only to find the doors closed, and dead-ends. It seems like no one understands that kind of hurt. It throbs, and we wonder if we'll ever walk tall again, or even walk at all.

But praise God there is healing for hurt! Jesus prayed alone in the garden in tears. God sustained him and He will sustain you because He cares about you. You are his special concern, and you are the "apple of His eye." God's answer to hurt is found in His Word:

13

The Lord your God is in your midst, a warrior who gives victory, He will rejoice over you with gladness, He will renew you in His love; He will exult over you with loud singing as on a day of festival. I will remove disaster from you, so that you will not bear reproach for it . . . at that time I will bring you home . . . (Zeph. 3:17, 18, 20).

Claim God's healing for your hurt, right now. Accept it as He waits to give it to you.

The woman had been caught in the very act of adultery. As if her self-image weren't low enough, the Pharisees made a public scene of her weakness. Her deliverance from hurt came the moment Jesus said to her; ". . . neither do I condemn you, go and sin no more!" You too, can be healed from hurt, regardless of the source of that hurt.

2

BYE BYE BITTERNESS

His face was stern. He shifted from one position to another as he sat across from my desk and related his inability to sleep, eat or have any peace or tranquility. He made good money, lived in a beautiful home, had a lovely wife, a secure job, and to top it all, could retire at least 7 years earlier than first expected. Looking at least ten years beyond his age, it was obvious to me that he was desperate. He wanted answers. With all the outward props of life in their proper place, why was he miserable, distraught, confused, and depressed? With only a little probing, the culprit was revealed: BITTERNESS!! Wronged in business fourteen years earlier, he had begun a new business career, but never had let go of the animosity he felt toward his old business partner. He was bound by bitterness . . . a bitterness that had been nursed and cultivated for 14 years. While outwardly he appeared successful, inwardly he was in shambles. He had already paid a high price for a low attitude.

He's not alone, is he? Unresolved bitterness and grudge have the effect of a fast spreading cancer; it eats you alive with no mercy. It really matters little whether the offense was small or large, a month ago or 14 years ago, whether the offender is blood related or is only a passing acquaintance, perpetuated bitterness binds you hand and foot. What poison does to the body, a held grudge does to the spirit. Those bound by a root of bitterness will pay a large price for their bondage. If nothing else, think what bitterness does . . . to you.

1. It prevents acceptable worship.

In the Sermon on the Mount, Jesus said something we would just as soon not hear! He warned that when you are offering your gift at the altar, and then remember that someone has something against you, leave your gift, go and set the record straight, then come and offer your gift (Matt. 5:23). It was the Lord's way of saying that relationships broken by misunderstanding or a held bitterness are barriers that keep us from worshiping God. Since worship is the highest thing we do, a held grudge keeps us from the highest calling in life. That's bondage!!

Notice in Jesus' instructions the conflict may not have begun with us, but with them. No matter!! The bottom line is, "get it straightened out!" Nowhere is getting rid of bitterness and conflict made clearer than right here.

2. It affects God's forgiveness of you.

In Mark 11:25, Jesus said; "And whenever you stand praying, forgive, if you have anything against anyone, so that your father also who is in heaven, may forgive you your trespasses." It is repeated in Matthew 6:14-15 as well as in Matthew 18:23-25. The presence of bitterness is refusal to forgive. Our refusal to forgive blocks God's forgiveness from our lives. That is not to say God is limited, it is to say that the only person God can't channel His mercy and pardon to is an unforgiving person. The spiritual disease of bitterness can bring spiritual death to us if left to occupy a place in our lives. This is serious. Why jeopardize our close fellowship with the Lord just for the luxury of harboring ill-will against someone else? It's truly a poor exchange.

3. It elevates you to a higher level than God!

Paul said it best. He admonishes us to forgive others, AS THE LORD HAS FORGIVEN YOU! (Eph. 4:32). Turned around, failure to forgive others makes us out to be greater than God. If God, who is wholly holy, totally pure, sovereign and supreme, is willing to forgive me, sinful and warped, who do I think I am to withhold forgiveness from others? Reason would state that I would have to be greater than God to do that!! Again, held-in bitterness derails our relationship with God.

4. It blocks your prayers.

Peter said it well. "Likewise you husbands, live considerately with your wives, . . . so that your prayers may not be hindered." Now you can't live considerately with someone if you're harboring and nursing bitterness, can you? The release of bitterness opens the prayer channel and makes it a clear channel. By the way, have you tried the secret of praying for the person to whom your bitterness is directed? You can't have bitterness long after you've prayed for them. Maybe it would be good for you to stop reading right now, and pray for that person!

Jesus knows us far better than we know ourselves. That's why He commanded us to "love our enemies, and pray for those who persecute us" (Matt. 5:44). A miracle takes place when we actually pray for the welfare and good of those against whom we harbor ill will. God changes us long before He changes them, but the marvelous thing is He changes both!!

5. It reconfirms that you don't love God.

That's a pretty strong statement to make, yet scripture bears it out. The sequence is clear. If we harbor bitterness and nurse a grudge, we obviously don't love the object of our bitterness. The Bible clearly states in I John 4:20; "If anyone says 'I love God' and hates his brother, he is a liar; for he who does not love his brother whom he has seen, cannot love God whom he has not seen." There is no justifiable way to tone that down. The continued presence of bitterness in our heart toward anyone reconfirms to us, to God, and to others, that we don't love that person . . . and if we don't love those whom we've seen and experienced, we can't love God whom we have not seen. One may object; "But it's easier to love God than it is to love those who have smeared my reputation or ruined my name among

17

friends." The fact is, however, if we can't love people on our own plane whom we see with our eyes and experience with other senses, it's hypocrisy to say we love God who is divine. But the presence of bitterness proves other things.

6. It proves you believe Jesus to be mistaken.

That's an even stronger statement, and it needs backing up. Now no one would come right out and say "I don't care what Jesus says, I'm not going to let go of this bitterness, because He could have been mistaken in what He said." What did He say at this point? "Then Peter came up and said to Him, 'Lord, how often shall my brother sin against me, and I forgive him? As many as seven times?' Jesus said to him, 'I do not say to you seven times, but seventy times seven'" (that doesn't mean when you have forgiven someone 490 times you are off the hook and don't have to forgive anymore!).

We not only have the privilege of forgiving and getting bitterness out of our life, we have a divine obligation to forgive. Jesus knew what the continued presence of unresolved bitterness and ill-will could do to us. That is why He spoke often and long about human relationships. Many who harbor and nurse grudges inside have either forgotten or never taken seriously the divine injunction to forgive, endlessly. Jesus taught this not for the sake of the offender, but for the sake of the offended. To go on and cultivate bitterness is to believe Jesus was mistaken in his teachings about endless forgiveness.

7. Unresolved bitterness brings a depression of spirit.

Those locked in the confines of bitterness are not happy, victorious people. You never hear anyone testify, "I'm still holding a grudge against so and so, and I'm so happy and living a great life of victory." No, the two are mutually exclusive. The Bible says, "A cheerful heart is a good medicine, but a downcast spirit dries up the bones" (Prov. 17:22). How true that is. Nothing breaks a spirit like a broken relationship whose parties refuse to reconnect. In fact, psychologists and counselors tell us today that one of the top three causes of acute depression is unresolved bitterness, often neatly tucked away in the subconscious.

8. Unresolved bitterness assumes a right we don't have.

We have the mistaken idea in our culture that when we've been offended, we have a granted right to get the offender back. It's here we love to press into action the "eye for an eye and tooth for a tooth" philosophy. "Nobody is going to do that to me and get away with it!" Sound familiar? It's said a million times a day by offended people. Much money and time are expended yearly in lawsuits and litigations to "get even." The fact is, those people never really "get even." They just get more confused and weary, and rightly so! Nowhere in the Bible are we bid to take vengeance upon ourselves personally. In fact, the contrary is commanded. "Beloved, never avenge yourselves, but leave it to the wrath of God; for it is written, 'Vengeance is mine, I will repay, says the Lord" (Rom. 12:19). When we assume a responsibility that isn't ours we're in trouble. I believe there are three reasons why God never wants us to assume the awesome responsibility of getting back. First, we never know all the facts. We may think we do, but we are always acting on partial information. You cannot administer proper justice with only part of the truth under your belt. Secondly, we cannot separate the offense from the offender. God hates the sin, but loves the sinner, He hates the offense, but loves the offender. We simply cannot make that separation. Thirdly, our attempts to get back are seldom, if ever, fair and just. We usually "botch" it up royally. That's why the Bible clearly says; "leave it . . . to the wrath of God" (Rom. 12:19). It's almost like the Bible is saying to us, "Leave it to the discretion of the Lord . . . He'll do it right, and His timing is impeccable."

By now, you're grimacing. Maybe you're saying, "Well, there are good reasons for not going back and making it right." What are your reasons? One I often hear is "It happened so long ago, it's best to let sleeping dogs lie." Whether it happened yesterday or 23 years ago, if it's unresolved, it's unresolved. In fact, the longer ago it happened is more reason to make it right since it's had the months and years to get encrusted. Bitterness breeds bitterness, and the longer we harbor it and nurse it, the deeply ingrained it becomes in our life. "But," maybe you're saying, "The one I'm harboring something against has moved away, they don't even live near here." The Bible didn't say for us to make it right only if they lived within so many miles! Distance is not a factor in righting wrongs between people.

The airlines will be happy to book you a reservation. Too expensive? Then what about the train, the bus, your car? Too much time? Then what about the U.S. Mail? Or what about your telephone? They even have special rates! Geographical distance doesn't stop us from paying bills or receiving payments. It doesn't stop us from sending Christmas presents or birthday cards. Why should it stop us from forgiving someone who has offended us?

"But . . . ," you may encounter, "it was a small offense, and it isn't worth the effort." Small or large, an offense is an offense, especially when it breaks a relationship. If someone cheated you out of $5 or $5000, there has been an offense, and usually the feelings run the same . . . they are feelings of anger, reaction, rebellion, and vengeance. When all other excuses have run their gamut, there is one last excuse; "The other person was in the wrong, and I feel it is their place to come and ask my forgiveness." Please don't forget . . . you are not responsible for their actions, but your own. Whether they ever come to you or not is outside your ability to control. You need to do something about that which you CAN do something about.

Bitterness is no respecter of class or age. Its binding power works among the young and the old. It happens inside families, companies, neighborhoods, and organizations, even "Christian" organizations. Maybe as you read this, you are bound by bitterness that has kept you captive for years. There is good news . . . Jesus not only wants to free you from that spirit of ill-will, He stands at your cell door with keys to unlock and let you out. You may walk out of that cell that has kept you bound, first by confessing it as a sin. Secondly, ask God for the wisdom needed for the best way of resolving the conflict. Pray for proper timing and circumstances. Thirdly, ACT. Go to the person, regardless of the cost in time, money, inconvenience. One of the heaviest weights that has ever been on your back will be removed and you'll be free to do anything God wants you to do. It's worth it!

3

WINNING OVER WORRY

Almost everyone has sat behind the bars of worry. This varmit is relentless and enslaving. You can find many definitions for worry, but the best comes from an Arkansas vegetable farmer; "Worry is gettin' all worked up over a bunch of stuff you ain't got no control over no way!" I think that really said it. No one can calculate the aspirins swallowed daily for throbbing headaches brought on by a worried mind. Worry truly is one responsibility God never intended us to assume. Worry greatly increases our ineffectiveness, our productiveness, and decreases our ability to cope with normal circumstances.

People worry over a number of things . . . money (or the lack of it), family members, marriages, jobs, grades, looks, etc. But one thing is clear, worry binds us like an oppression that grips and imprisons to keep us from being all we were meant to be and do all we were meant to do.

I'll never forget reading about the man who decided to visit a counselor about his worrying problem. The counselor gave some wise counseling. He advised the man to set aside an afternoon, one day a week to do his worrying, and save all his worries for that one day and afternoon. He selected Thursday afternoon. At work on Monday morning before the coffee break he began to worry; He wrote his worry down and filed it in the Thursday afternoon file. All day, he dropped "worry memos" in the file. All week, the file became thicker and thicker, but he didn't worry because he had an appointment set for that . . . afternoon. Thursday finally arrived. At the stroke of noon he headed for his file, looked under W, and, oops! The worry file was missing. He looked and looked, but it was gone. He sat down to try to reconstruct all the things he was supposed to worry about. He couldn't remember one, not even one! His problem was solved. The poet said it well:

> SOME OF THE HURTS YOU HAVE CURED
> AND THE SHARPEST YOU STILL HAVE SURVIVED,
> BUT WHAT TORMENTS OF GRIEF YOU'VE ENDURED
> FROM THE EVILS THAT NEVER ARRIVED!

Worry is fretting and stewing over (1) things that haven't happened yet, (2) things over which we have no control to change, and (3) things that are basically unknown. If we can do something about a situation, we need to do it. If we can't we need to leave it. In either case, there is no call or need for worry.

How can we be set free from worry and anxiety? Freedom comes in remembering 7 life-changing truths!

1. YOU HAVE WORTH AND VALUE TO GOD. You count, you matter, you're valuable to the Lord whether you know it or not. Jesus warned us; "Do not be anxious about your life, what you shall eat or what you shall drink, nor about your body, what you shall put on. Is not life more than food and the body more than clothing? Look at the birds of the air; they neither sow nor reap nor gather into barns, and yet your heavenly father feeds them. "Are you not of more value than they?" (Matt. 6:25-26). That last question is a key to your freedom from worry! You are more valuable to God than any other part of His creation. Jesus went on to say to consider the lilies of the field, how they grow, they neither toil nor spin, yet nothing is arrayed like they. If God feeds the birds and makes the flowers beautiful, what do we have to worry about, we who are the highest form of His glorious creation?

SAID THE ROBIN TO THE SPARROW: "I WOULD REALLY LIKE
TO KNOW, WHY THESE HUMANS RUSH AROUND AND WORRY
SO." SAID THE SPARROW TO THE ROBIN, "I REALLY THINK THAT
IT MUST BE, THEY HAVE NO HEAVENLY FATHER, LIKE YOU
AND ME." Wow, that really says it for us, doesn't it? The first key
to freedom from the bondage of worry is remembering your worth
and value to God.

2. WORRY CHANGES NOTHING, EXCEPT YOUR LIFE FOR THE
WORSE! It's true, Jesus said it better than anyone; "And which of
you by being anxious can add one cubit to his span of life?" (Matt.
6:27). All the furrowed foreheads, the pacing, the twiddling of the
thumbs and the clenching of fists have never changed one thing . . .
except the worrier, it usually made him sick! If everyone could preface
their worry project with this question; "What will I accomplish by
doing this worrying?" it would stop the process fairly fast. Anxiety
never changed a thing for the better.

3. WORRY IS A POOR WITNESS. Have you ever thought how
others see your anxiety? Since it doesn't glorify God or promote
His kingdom, it is an extremely poor witness. Jesus went on to say
in the 6th chapter of Matthew; "Therefore do not be anxious saying
'What shall we eat? or What shall we drink? or What shall we wear?
For the Gentiles seek all these things. . . .' " Jesus made it clear that
it's the heathen who worry, fret, stew and fuss over things. Jesus
made it clear that His followers were different. Worry before an
unbelieving world says, in so many words, we don't believe God is
able! The presence of worry is usually the absence of faith. Before
the eyes of the unbelieving world, a worrying Christian is a vote against
Christianity.

4. REMEMBER TO LIVE ONE DAY AT A TIME! That's how to
handle the problem of worry. Jesus said; "Therefore, do not be
anxious about tomorrow, for tomorrow will be anxious for itself.
Let the day's own trouble be sufficient for the day" (Matt. 6:34).
We have all heard about the mathematical clock who, one day, calcu-
lated how many times a day it ticked, then just stopped from sheer
exhaustion! The old wise grandfather clock nearby gave good words
of wisdom, "Take one tick at a time." Jesus' wise words are not
tantamount to a philosophy of making no plans, setting no goals, or
being undisciplined in preparation. What He is saying is, don't

borrow difficulties, problems, knotty situations and roadblocks from tomorrow. Man was created to handle the difficulties of today, not tomorrow or next month!

5. NOTHING QUALIFIES TO BE WORTHY ENOUGH FOR WORRY! If we could only remember that, it would cut from our lives 95% of all worry. Nothing is worth worrying over. Paul drove this point home for us vividly; "Have no anxiety about anything, but by prayer and supplication, let your request be made known to God. And the peace of God which passes all understanding will keep your hearts and minds in Christ Jesus" (Phil. 4:6-7). Wow! What an admonition! Now notice something. He didn't say "have no anxiety about most things." Nor did he say "have little anxiety about anything." Nor did he say, "have some anxiety about a few things." HAVE NO ANXIETY ABOUT ANYTHING! No anxiety means zero. Anything means any-thing. Nothing is worthy of worry. If it's big enough to worry about, it belongs in God's department. If it's a very small thing, He's probably given you the wherewithal to handle it. In either case, it doesn't qualify for worry.

6. OBJECTS OF WORRY ARE ALWAYS TEMPORARY. A good example of this is given for us in Psalm 37. David exhorts us not to fret over the wicked who always seem to get ahead. It seems they prosper. As David put it in Psalm 73 "For they have no pangs; their bodies are sound and sleak, they are not in trouble as other men are; they are not stricken like other men" (Ps. 73:4-5). Then back in Psalm 37, he points out their transient nature; "For they will soon fade like the grass, and wither like the green herb" (Ps. 37:2). Again ". . . Fret not yourself, it tends only to evil. For the wicked shall be cut off; . . . yet a little while, and the wicked will be no more; though you look well at his place, he will not be here" (Ps. 37:8b-10). Several other verses in that Psalm highlight the fact that those over whom we fret aren't going to last. So . . . why worry over them, why fret, why stew over their very temporary success? There is a godly principle here we need to heed. Everything we worry over is a situation that won't last. Even if it did, worry is futile and destructive.

7. THERE IS A GOOD DUMPING GROUND FOR WORRY—AVAIL YOURSELF OF IT. God has not only forbidden us to worry, and shown us its futility, He's provided a place we can file every worry and anxiety. In I Peter 5:7, the Bible says; "Cast all your care on Him,

because he cares about you." J.B. Phillips has captured the meaning of this in his modern English translation. "YOU CAN THROW THE WHOLE WEIGHT OF YOUR ANXIETIES ON HIM, FOR YOU ARE HIS PERSONAL CONCERN." What a promise! What a provision! What a plan! It is indeed in this passage we find the key of release from worry and anxiety. Maybe you are the proverbial "worry-wart." Those bound in the hand-cuffs of worry are not free to be victorious, happy, or productive. Worry drains you of energy, creativity, and strips you of the life-style Jesus died for you to have. He who broke the bonds of death, and is alive today, stands before your worry-laden life to say; YOU'RE FREE TO GO NOW! Why not pray this prayer of release, right now?

> Dear God, I confess my sin of worry. I confess that it casts doubts upon your interest and concern for me as your child. I confess that it has drained my energy, robbed me of joy, and brought emotional and sometimes physical illness to my life.
>
> Right now, I release my worry to you, casting on you my anxieties and frettings. I accept your deliverance. Amen.

Remember, Satan can render the strongest Christian ineffective and unfruitful if he can develop a worried mind in you. Here is where we need to stand, verbally and with authority, against Satan. Left un-checked and un-abandoned, worry will even bring on physical illness that can result in sure death. Confess your worry as sin, abandon it, and trust the sovereignty of God. It works!

4

NOBODY NEEDS TO BE NOBODY

It happened at a fast-food chain. When I gave my order, paid for my food, after giving me my change, the matter-of-fact clerk said with a mechanical coldness, "You're number 18." I took my receipt with 18 scribbled on the back and sat down to wait. I mused to myself, "Is that all I am? A number?" Has life been reduced to a number only? It seems I've been assigned numbers all my life. At birth, I was baby number 4 on that day. I weighed in at 8-1/2 pounds and was 21 inches long. Every birthday brings a new number to remember. Then I'm identified with an area code number, a phone number, social security number, a zip code number, a P.O. Box number, a street number, apartment number, a driver's license number, and now I can't even get a bite to eat without being given a number again. It's enough to make you cry out, "Am I more than just a number?"

Millions today suffer much in the prison house of inferiority. It is a bondage that defaces us as God-created beings. It's the mind-set and attitude that says, "I don't count, I'm not important, I don't matter, I'm nothing, I have nothing to offer, I'm insignificant, I'm really just a nobody in a world of somebodies." Many seek to sanctify such a mood by calling it great humility. Now, I'm aware that the Bible says we are not to think of ourselves more highly than we ought to think, but that doesn't mean we're nobodies. True inferiority is not a psychological problem, nor even a social problem, it is a spiritual problem. If we treat it superficially we will get superficial and very temporary results. If we go to the root of the attitude and face it as sin, the Lord will bring a permanent deliverance and free us from its debilitating and diabolical effects.

There is much in our world that tends to reduce us to the level of "nobodies." It is a world of high and rising technology. Knowledge and wisdom are changing so rapidly even sophisticated computers cannot keep up. Publishers of books containing facts about our world and its trends and events are outdated before the ink is dry. In industry people are devastated when one machine or one robot replaces 5 workers. It threatens our very identity, and tends to reduce us to nobodies in a world of high tech.

Job security (or job insecurity) is another breeder of inferiority. Thirty-five years ago 79% of men who chose a career stayed with that career on to and through retirement. Today is another story. Close to 83% of adult males in America will make at least one major career change before they're 35 years old! Those kinds of changes, with a family, rate a high score on the stress chart. It forces one to think "Is anything for sure?" This question tends to promote an inferiority syndrome that says, "Maybe I'm no good at what I'm doing."

The mobility of our society is a major contributor to feelings of inferiority. People move more than ever. Roots have all but become a thing of the past. Very few children grow up where they will eventually live, and very few grow up around grandparents. Mobilization has a way of manufacturing impersonalization. No one makes deep friendships in neighborhoods, because they know in just a few months or years they will be moving on. The increasing number of high-security condominium and apartment complexes has fostered this impersonal mind set. Few apartment dwellers even know the names of those who live on the other side of their kitchen wall!

The shrinking world coupled with living under the threat of total annihilation by thermonuclear power tends to awe people into inferiority. And the list goes on. The bottom line, however, is that too many,

Christian and non Christian, feel inadequate, inferior, sub-acceptable, and often worthless. If we aren't careful, we can all get the "grasshopper blues." That's what happened to the people sent up to spy out the land of Canaan. They came back with glowing reports of a "land flowing with milk and honey." But with lips down to their knees, they said, "The Anakim (giants) were there . . . and we seemed to them like grasshoppers, and so we seemed to ourselves" (Num. 13:33). Once you fall behind the bars of inferiority, it's hard to lose the grasshopper syndrome. It is indeed a debilitating bondage in that it reduces us to so much less than what God made us to be! In 1879, a Jewish child was born, a son of a poor merchant. In his early years he became withdrawn because of the anti-semitic feelings of his day. He was so shy and quiet, inhibited in learning, his parents had him examined to see if he was normal. He failed his entrance exams to college in Zurich, Switzerland in 1895. Finally graduating with a doctor's degree, he accepted an obscure job as a patent examiner in the Bern patent office. One day he was seized with an idea called "relativity." Albert Einstein abandoned all else to give himself to his idea, which he called something greater than his life. Nobody needs to be a nobody, and nobody needs to stay a nobody.

How may we be freed from the imprisonment of inferiority? These steps will free us.

STEP #1 DON'T FORGET YOUR HERITAGE! In essence this is what Mordecai said to Esther when the lives of the whole Jewish nation were in her hand. "Who knows," exhorted Mordecai to Esther, "whether you have not come to the kingdom for such a time as this?" (Esther 4:14). Remember who you are! You're a chosen vessel of God, a Jew, don't forget your heritage. We need to remind ourselves often that we are God's highest creation. He capped off all created things with man.

STEP #2 DON'T FORGET YOUR UNIQUENESS! Inferiority often comes when people begin thinking they're just another number, another statistic, another consumer. Not so! The Bible teaches that you are special, uniquely created with abilities, traits, gifts, and talents no one else exactly shares. The Psalmist said it best in his prayer of transparency:

Thou didst form my inward parts, thou didst knit me together in my mother's womb. I praise thee for thou art fearful and wonderful . . .

29

thou knowest me right well; my frame was not hidden from thee, when I was being made in secret, intricately wrought in the depths of the earth. Thy eyes beheld my unformed substance; in thy book were written everyone of them, the days that were formed for me, when as yet there was none of them (Ps. 139:13-16).

How could it be said any better? God planned you, you didn't just happen. He created you differently than anyone else. Your very metabolism is different, your brain waves are different, your fingerprints match no other human's on earth! Feelings of inferiority become a denial of Sovereign planning! Saul in the Old Testament almost missed being king because of inferior feelings. During the kingly coronation ceremonies, when they were ready for the anointed man of God to take his place and assume his authority before the people, the Bible says, ". . . but when they sought him, he could not be found . . . and the Lord said, 'Behold, he has hidden himself among the baggage' " (I Sam. 10:21, 22). Imagine that! Hadn't he been anointed? Yes. Hadn't he been promised that the Spirit of the Lord would come upon him and that he would be turned into another man (I Sam. 10:9)? Yes! Then, what is this picture of a tall, handsome, young and able man . . . hiding in a pile of suitcases? It is the picture of what the bondage of inferiority can do.

There is no telling how much potential is locked up and sealed among God's people today because they feel they're nobodies in a world of somebodies. Not until you realize that you have been specially made, uniquely created, and that you are an "original" will you be free to become all God made you to become.

STEP #3 DON'T FORGET THE SUPERNATURAL! Have you ever asked, "What was it that made those eleven cowardly, fearful, groping, inhibited men we call apostles, spiritual giants?" From men who all forsook Jesus and fled, to men who turned the world upside down was quite a transformation. They outlived, out-prayed, out-gave, out-worked, out-ran, and out-stayed their Roman pagan contemporaries only because they were plugged into the supernatural. By nature they were frail, and quite inferior. But something happened. It was said "Now when they saw the boldness of Peter and John, and perceived that they were uneducated, common men, they wondered." If that's as far as you read, you would wonder too! But the very next sentence says, ". . . and they recognized that they had been with

Jesus'' (Acts 4:13). That was the key. They rose above their inferiority by plugging into the supernatural. Indeed, ordinary men without the clout of position, education, money or human cleverness did extra-ordinary things in extra-ordinary ways, because they had been with Jesus! No matter which way you slice it, it comes out with one conclusion. In Jesus Christ you become somebody. That's why Paul wrote, "and you have come to fullness of life in Him . . ." (Col. 2:10).

Peter wrote to some scattered believers in A.D. 63. They had been uprooted by persecution; they were homeless; some had been physically abused by the enemy. They were discouraged, and began to wonder if it was worth it all. It was not enough for Peter to tell them that what they were experiencing was normal for the Christian. Feeling like a bunch of nobodies, they needed to know they counted, they mattered, that they were important. So he wrote these words to them:

> But you are a CHOSEN RACE, A ROYAL PRIESTHOOD, A HOLY NATION, GOD'S OWN PEOPLE . . . once you were no people, but now you are God's people (I Peter 2:9-10).

This was the Holy Spirit's way of saying, "Before Christ you didn't have a sense of worth, a sense of belonging, a sense of being someone; but now that's all changed."

Maybe the most profound example of coming from nobodies to somebodies is the children of Israel in the Old Testament. They had wandered in the wilderness, yet somehow believed they were God's chosen people. Yet they were discouraged. They had hoped for so much, yet so little had come. Their mood was reflected in the spies that were sent from Paran to Canaan to spy out the promised land. There were twelve of them. Those spies found a land flowing with milk and honey (silk and money). The land was lush, rich in every way. There was only one "fly in the ointment." They met the Hittites, Jebusites and Amorites. They came back insisting that the possessors of the land were giants. They also confessed, ". . . and we seemed to ourselves like grasshoppers, and so we seemed to them" (Num. 13:33). Talk about inferiority, you can't go much lower than that. Grasshoppers! Is that what we are? Truly, those Jews had magnified their difficulties, and minimized their resource, God! Don't we all tend to do that? No, they didn't need glasses, they needed vision within. Maybe you've "seemed" like a grasshopper lately. Maybe "they" seem like giants. Take heart, you can be free from "seeming" and "feeling" less than you are. Will you pray this prayer and mean it?

31

Dear God,

I may be vanilla, but I'm made of real cream! Today, I confess my position in You, blood-bought, Spirit-filled, an heir, a child of the King, saved and kept. Oh Lord, amidst the demeaning dreariness of my seemingly dwarfed significance, remind me that He that is in me is greater than he that is in the world. Strip me of all that would remind me that I'm valueless, cheap and insignificant. Remind me that with You I count, I matter, that I'm important, yes, even essential to your cause. In a world where everything is measured in size, in weight, and in monetary value, remind me that in your Kingdom, things are measured differently. Deliver me from the deadliness of a do-nothing attitude. Reinforce me with a sense of worth, of value, of importance. While I will never stand before throngs, or sing before royalty, or march before dignitaries, or perform before kings, I'm vital to your Kingdom, Lord, because no organ or limb is unimportant to the body. Lord, I'm not unimportant to you. And Lord, though "vanilla," I'm willing to be topped with all your goodies and toppings that will make me colorful and tasteful to those with whom and to whom I minister.

Amen.

Yes, you count, you matter, you have unique significance to God. You may FEEL like a nobody, but let no one tell you you're nobody. God says you're somebody! In Christ we're royalty, and someday will come into the full inheritance. You can count on it!

5

DELIVERED FROM DEPRESSION

One man who was hopelessly caught in the web of depression said, "The only light at the end of the tunnel is a locomotive doing 70 mph trying to run you down." It doesn't take long to diagnose depression. The outward symptoms are clear: exhaustion, some insomnia, withdrawal from people, poor eating habits, low energy, loss of anticipation which is often accompanied by a listless spirit.

Helen, (not her real name), seemed always bubbly. She walked with a bounce, her eyes were bright, her smile broad, and her voice cheery. You can imagine my surprise when she sat down in my study and said, "Let's get right to the point . . . I'm terribly depressed." There were no tears, no frowns, no emotional outbursts, but a cold matter-of-factness that was almost void of the usual warmth she exuded. I thought inwardly, "Surely not you, of all people, not the lady who cheers everyone up when she walks down the hallway!" But it was she, and she was depressed. I started where every counselor starts, recounting past events, happenings, experiences and changes that could have brought it all on. Not a clue. In fact, part of Helen's depression stemmed from the fact that she could find no catastrophic event or events to which she could tie her depression. One thing is clear about depression. Its cause is probably the hardest thing in the world to discover. Often, it isn't one thing, but a series of things, or a life pattern of attitude that brings on chronic depression.

In some instances, depression can be traced to a physical cause. Sometimes, imbalanced hormones, a metabolism that's off, high blood pressure, recurring pain, or terminal illness can bring on depression. Job surely linked some of his depression to a physical cause. He wrote:

> "Has not a man a hard service upon earth, and are not his days like the days of a hireling? Like a slave who longs for the shadow and like a hireling who looks for his wages, so I am allotted months of emptiness and nights of misery are apportioned to me. When I lie down, I say 'When shall I arise?' But the night is long, and I am full of tossings till the dawn. My flesh is clothed with worms and dirt, my skin hardens then breaks out afresh. My days are swifter than a weaver's shuttle, and come to the end without hope" (Job. 7:1-6).

Job has said it for many who find themselves locked in the vice of haunting and debilitating depression. How we respond to illness determines whether it will cause depression or not. Someone has said there are two ways to catch a dagger; we can catch it by the blade and be severely cut, or we can catch it by the handle and use it. Have you noticed how some people are perennially sick? Today it's a cold, next week it's the flu, next month it's stomach problems, then headaches set in, then the whole cycle begins over. In some cases, (I repeat, SOME cases), some people are sick most of the time because they confess sickness, they are oriented toward sickness, they visualize sickness, are programmed for sickness, so they are sick. On the other hand, a great many (not all) people who are perennially healthy are people who confess health, believe health, behave healthy, and they are healthy. Again, I'm not ignoring real organic illness. It comes, even to people usually healthy, but attitude makes the difference. It also makes a difference how you respond to illness when it does come. Job gave in to it, thus it drove him to more depression and loneliness. So it would be more accurate to say that some depression comes because we have responded to illness negatively, without faith that God can deliver, and until He does deliver, has the ability to use even the sickness to make us stronger and to glorify Himself.

Sometimes depression comes from unresolved guilt. Underscore the word, UNRESOLVED! Guilt is a wonderful gift from God. It's like fever. Fever isn't an illness, but a warning bell that something is wrong inside. Thus guilt is an indicator that something is partially wrong inside. We can do a number of things with this "early warning system" called guilt. We can deny it is there and go on. We can suppress it with some kind of lid and keep it under cover. We can apply human "remedies" such as trying to drown it with alcohol, curb its sting with pills, assuage its pricking with ungodly counsel. But guilt, left unresolved, can do a disastrous number on us. King David knew this from experience. After he had committed adultery with Bathsheba, murdered her husband, then lied to cover it up, he became miserable. Listen to his own words of what happened before he finally confessed it to God:

> When I declared not my sin, my body wasted away through my groaning all day long. For day and night thy hand was heavy upon me; my strength was dried up as by the heat of summer (Ps. 32:3-4).

David was miserable. He couldn't sleep, or eat, or think straight. Finally, when he could no longer cope, he did the right thing which he should have done first, he confessed!

> I acknowledged my sin to thee, and I did not hide my iniquity; I said I will confess my transgressions to the Lord, *THEN* (italics mine), thou didst forgive the guilt of my sin (Ps. 32:5).

Notice the timing: it wasn't until David confessed that cleansing came and the pressure was lifted. The catharsis of a broken, contrite, penitent heart brought wholeness. David then was free! Maybe even now as you read this you are suffering from depression, and yet like Helen, everything has been going great, there seems to be no cause. Could it be that in some area of your life you haven't come clean with God in contrite confession of sin? He's more willing to cleanse than we are to ask for that cleansing.

Sometimes depression is a special delivery letter direct from Satan to oppress us. The Psalmist again said, "Why go I mourning because of the oppression of the enemy?" (Ps. 43:2). Satan's sharpest tool, I'm convinced, is discouragement and depression. If he can oppress believers with the spirit of depression, he will help confirm to the world that one's faith in Christ is woefully inadequate to take one through all the exigencies of life. Believe me, he uses this tool whenever and wherever there is an opening!

Elijah was severely depressed. The evil spirit of Jezebel devastated this strong prophet of God. All of this occurred after a signal victory. Elijah had just come off the greatest victory of his life . . . the test of Mount Carmel between the Baals and God. Four hundred and fifty prophets of Baal were defeated and killed. God's power was greater than Baal's power! This victory should have brought joy to Elijah. But a single threat of the woman Jezebel caused Elijah to crash and burn. He sat down under a broom tree. (Be careful about sitting under broom trees, or you will be swept away!) Elijah was so depressed that he prayed for God to take his life. Upon an angel's message, Elijah rose and ate and went on for another forty days. They must have been miserable days, however, because when they came to an end, Elijah found himself in a cave. It seemed to be all over. Elijah had quit, pulled up and parked on a dead-end street. It was here (I Kings 19:9) that God spoke to Elijah and said, "What are you doing here Elijah? You . . . you, Elijah, of all people, the one I've anointed, the one I've empowered, the one to whom I've given victory and authority . . . what are YOU doing here?" It was then that God assured him that he had preserved 7000 people who had not bowed the knee to Baal. God had to assure him He was still God.

Now, what can we say was the CAUSE of Elijah's depression? I think it was poor theology! Poor theology? Yes. Elijah had allowed his God to shrink to the place where he was no longer sovereign and in total control. Jezebel's threat was, in Elijah's eyes, bigger than God's power, so he succumbed to depression.

How big is your God? He is sovereign or He isn't God. He is the God who said, "Is anything too hard for me?" (Jer. 32:27). Depression often comes when we feel God is no longer at the controls.

Enough of the cause, what about the cure? There is a way out. The following Biblical principles, if followed, will bring you out of depression.

1. ACKNOWLEDGE THE SOURCE OF MOST DEPRESSION

We've already seen the source. God is not the author of depression. God does not want you to live a defeated, discouraged and depressing life. If God is not the author, Satan is. Jesus told a parable about a man who sowed good seed in his field. While men slept, his enemy came and sowed weeds among the wheat. When the wheat came up, so did the weeds. Note, none really saw them sow the bad seed. That's how it is with depression; you may never know the exact minute, or day, or hour Satan sows that ugly debilitating seed in your life. You might remember in that parable in Matthew 13:24-30 that the householder knew immediately that the source of the problem had come from the enemy. That's the first step in ridding your life of depression. It's not from God, but from Satan. By the way, Jesus made it clear who sowed the bad seed; ". . . the weeds are the sons of the evil one, and the enemy who sowed them is the devil" (Matt. 13:38b-39a). So the first step is to acknowledge the source and confess that because it came from the enemy it doesn't belong in your life.

2. CLAIM WHAT YOU HAVE!

In I John 4:4, the Bible says, "Little children, you are of God and have overcome them, for he who is in you is greater than he who is in the world." What a truth!! What a relief!! What an assurance!! If the first step is to acknowledge the source, which is Satan, the second step is to acknowledge our authority over him. We have in us Him who is greater than he who is in the world, Satan. If the source is Satan, the resource is Jesus Christ. Thus, the resource is greater than the source. Believe me, just confessing that over and over is enough to catapult you out of depression for good!!

3. CONFESS YOUR VICTORY NOW!

Maybe you're saying, "Isn't that a little premature?" NO! Don't wait until you feel good about shouting victory, shout victory regardless of your feelings. Again, the Psalmist said with confidence:

> My God in His steadfast love will meet me; My God will let me look
> in triumph over my enemies (Ps. 59:10).

It's not easy to confess victory when you know that so many stand against you. But victory is easily confessed when we read:

> . . . This I know, that God is for me (Ps. 56:9b).

What a statement; what a consoling truth. God is for me. That is the commitment my God and your God has made to us. Jude 24 says,

". . . He is able to keep you from falling. . . ." I hold onto that verse in times of great stress and when discouragement lurks to steal my joy.

4. OFFER YOUR DEPRESSION TO GOD!

Like a traveler turns over his luggage to the bellhop, we need to surrender our depression to God. He really desires to take it away from us so that we can be all He's created us to be.

> Cast your burden on the Lord and He will sustain you; he will never permit the righteous to be moved (Ps. 55:22).

There is a command and a promise. The command is to cast. The promise is that He will keep us solidly anchored so we won't be blown away by the wind of adversity or grief. That's why Peter could say what he said:

> Cast all your anxieties on Him because He cares about you (I Peter 5:7).

I have found it to be very effective that when I'm offering anything over to God, to find a secluded place, stand in that place, and with uplifted hands, as though I'm handing a board to a carpenter above me, say to God; "God I give up this depression to you, I relinquish it and confess it gone!" It works, try it!!

5. PRAISE GOD IN ADVANCE FOR DELIVERANCE

There is an amazing power in praise. The tallest we'll ever stand and strongest we'll ever be is when we are praising God, especially in advance of His seen action. A good example of this is found in Jehoshaphat. When multitudes of the enemy headed his way, he sought the Lord immediately before he sought anything else. But there is one verse in that whole account that is arresting! The enemy was pursuing. By a million to one, Jehoshaphat's army, humanly speaking, were about to be "goners." There were no time outs and it was the last minute of the last quarter and the score was 0 to 0. It was not the time to try unproven plays. Notice what they did:

> And when they began to sing and praise, the Lord set an ambush against the men of Ammon, Moab, and Mount Seir who had come against Judah, so that they were routed (II Chron. 20:22).

Did you notice when the Lord intervened? The timing is impeccable. It happened exactly when they began to sing and praise. Hope is more than whistling in the dark. It always anticipates the future. Hope is not concerned with the present. The Bible says we have been born anew to a "living hope" (I Peter 1:3). That living hope is based and anchored on the Word of God. It's not shaky. We can stand secure on that hope. How? If you want out of depression, you must have a vision of yourself, care-free, joyful, excited, up, and moving. Picture yourself in that frame of mind and life, then agree with God that that is a reality. This is not some cheap name it and claim it theology; hope is very real. No one hopes without a vision. If you visualize defeat and morbidity for the future, that's what you'll experience. How much better to experience the other!

Never allow circumstances to hinder you from creativity or to color your mood. A time of trouble is a time to prepare for renewal in life. John Milton's greatest work was done amidst the chaos of England's Civil War. Bunyan's *Pilgrim's Progress* came from Bedford Prison and the hurt of man's intolerance. Byron, Keats, and Shelley wrote while France and England were locked in war; and Goethe wrote himself into immortality while Napoleon's armies were marching across Europe. Abraham Lincoln insisted that the reconstruction of the Capitol go on even through the dark hours of war. Even in the midst of depression, we need to go on, hold our head high, believe God, and trust for total deliverance. It will come.

If God can cause the walls of Jericho to tumble by a seven day march, if He can part the Red Sea, heal a leper by dipping in water seven times, if He can raise the dead, and bring creation out of nothing, He can deliver you from your depression. Why not pray this prayer right now?

GOD, I ACCEPT YOUR DELIVERANCE FROM DEPRESSION THIS VERY MOMENT. THOUGH YOU DIDN'T SEND IT, YOU HAVE POWER TO REMOVE IT. I NOW CLAIM THAT POWER, AND BELIEVE IT DONE! AMEN.

6

LOOSED FROM LUST

Tony had been a Christian for only three months. Tall, muscular, extremely handsome, he sat on the edge of the sofa. "I'll get right to the point . . . I've got a severe problem with lust!" I thought to myself, "that's somewhat normal for a young 25-year-old single man." But Tony went on to relate an attitude and pattern of life that haunted him since he was 17 years old. Like many young men outside of Christ, he had delved into the world of the lust of the flesh and had emerged hooked. Like a fire burning within him, there seemed to be no extinguisher to snuff the flames. Even as a Christian, Tony was locked into sexual lust and couldn't seem to find the key to extricate himself. Though embarrassed, he desperately wanted out.

We live in a society tainted with sex. Madison Avenue has learned that sex sells. It sells cars, soap, perfume, aftershave, deodorant, clothes, and you name it. It's splashed on billboards, inked in newspapers, seen on T. V., heard on radio, photographed on calendars. The fact is, it's hard to escape. Tony's problem isn't isolated or unusual.

We tend to forget that God created sex, but called for it to operate within the confines of marital love. Man has taken God's creation, twisted it, warped it, and perverted something very beautiful into a monster that seeks to control.

One thing we need to realize. When we became Christians, we died to sin (Rom. 6:2). The old Adamic nature in us died. It didn't get sick, it DIED, DEAD! That does not mean our struggle with sin is over, because sin still operates in the sphere of our physical bodies and minds, though it has been eradicated from our spirits. Paul reminds us also in Romans 6 that sin will have no dominion over us. In other words, we don't have to obey the taskmaster of sin anymore, yet we find ourselves slipping and doing just that. Is there really deliverance from sexual lust? Or must you spend the rest of your life struggling as a victim of your lower nature? The answer comes in knowing what we are made of, knowing who we are, and knowing what God's word promises. Where do we start? I believe there are 7 steps to victory in overcoming lust.

1. KNOW THE SOURCE OF LUST.

Does it just drop down out of the air to plague us? Do we inherit it from our parents? Are we taught it? Where does it come from? The Bible says:

> For from within, out of the heart of man, come evil thoughts, forni-cation, theft, murder, adultery, coveting, wickedness, deceit, licentious-ness, wickedness, slander, pride, and foolishness. All these evil things come from within, and they defile a man (Mark 7:21-23).

Jesus put his finger on the source. Lust springs from the flesh part of man, from what Paul called the body of sin. It's from within, but triggered by what is without. It really begins in the mind, though that is usually not where it ends. Of course, we don't have to guess who put it in the mind. Satan's mission is to deceive us, and he does this through our thinking. Your mind is the battlefield between Satan and good. The war is won or lost there, not in the members of your body.

2. CONFESS LUST AS SIN.

Lust is not a psychological problem, it's not an emotional problem, not even a genetic problem. It is a spiritual problem. It is sin. Sin can

42

be covered up, rationalized away, drowned in alcohol, denied, or confessed. God's remedy is confession. Confession is done, not just so we can experience God's cleansing and forgiveness, but also to drive home to us that the problem is spiritual. It's amazing today that when a horrible sex crime is committed, the standard remark is, "What a sickness." This is society's way of writing it all off as a sickness. It is a sin, not a sickness. Now sin makes us sick in thought, word and deed, but in its origin it is sin. Note what the Bible says:

> Do not love the world, nor the things in the world. If anyone loves the world, the love of the Father is not in him. For all that is in the world, the lust of the flesh, and the lust of the eyes, and the boastful pride of life is not of the Father, but is of the world (I John 2:15-16).

Now notice that John talks about two kinds of lust. He talks about the lust of the flesh. Then he talks about the lust of the eyes. The word lust in the New Testament is also translated desire. So the process is that we see it, we think about it, then we do it, that is, if it follows the normal course. Here, John identifies lust as sin, and we need to do the same. To evade the fact that it's a sin problem is to evade the real issue. Ours is an age that delights in relabeling sin to reduce its harshness. The encroachment of humanism has hoodwinked many into believing problems caused by sin have their root in something else. For example, you often hear it said of a rapist, "He's a very sick man." Or you hear people say of a mass murderer, "A person would have to be out of his mind to do something like that." Our tendency is to ascribe the cause of people's behavior to something other than a spiritual problem. To be sure, there are some cases of severe mental illness, but it's time we started calling sin what it is, SIN. When a bankrobber robs, he sins. When a violent man injures another, he sins. When a person commits illicit sex, he sins. The Bible makes it clear that perennial lust is sin. It's not a mental problem, or sociological problem, or genetic problem, or emotional problem, it is a sin problem. Deliverance from lust will never come till we face it for what it is and acknowledge its source.

3. CONFESS IT TO A TRUSTED FELLOW BELIEVER.

The Bibles makes that pretty plain:

> Confess your sins to one another, and pray for one another, that you may be healed (James 5:16).

Vertical confession isn't enough. The Bible teaches us to confess our sins to one another. Some shrink back in horror and say, "That could be dangerous!" But that is man's way of looking at it. God said do it, so we ought to do it. Why? Familial confession to a trusted believer can grant the opportunity for someone else to hold you up in prayer besides yourself. That's why the Bible further says:

> Therefore encourage one another and build one another up, just as you are doing (I Thess. 5:11).

The ministry of encouragement is so vital when we are talking about deliverance from lust. Also, there is an element of accountability. We need our feet held to the fire. We need a trusted fellow believer to say occasionally, "How's it going today?" Maybe your resistance to this comes at the point of a myth we have fostered and fed through the years as Christians. It is the myth that says, "If others know I have a weakness, they may think less of me, and wonder what else I'm not telling." It's too bad we have fostered in our culture a "macho" mentality . . . an attitude that projects the idea that I've got everything together, no chinks in the armor, no cracks, no flaws, everything is in apple pie order!! That is spiritual nonsense! Why do you think the Bible says:

> Bear one another's burden and so fulfill the law of Christ (Gal. 6:2).

Now note, I said to confess your lust to a TRUSTED believer. I don't think God wants us to parade our dirty laundry to the public in general. But neither does He want us to carry around our necks a load we were never built to carry.

4. KNOW GOD'S WILL FOR YOU IN THIS AREA.

Many people are breaking their necks to discover the "will of God" for their lives. Yet in the Word of God, God has made known His will for us clearly. Some, locked in the log-jam of lust simply throw up their hands and say, "Well, I guess there's no escape, this is the way God made me, and I've got to live with it." WRONG! The Bible says clearly:

> For this is the will of God, your sanctification; that you abstain from unchastity; that each one of you know how to take a wife for himself, in holiness and honor, NOT IN THE PASSION OF LUST like the heathen who do not know God (I Thess. 4:3-5).

God has called us to holiness. Positional holiness comes when we accept Jesus Christ into our lives as our personal Saviour and Lord. Practical holiness comes as an outgrowth of that vertical relationship. Holy living, pure living, clean living, is God's plan for our lives. So many are living contrary to the best God planned for them. What God wills, God has the power to bring about. If He wills your deliverance from a lustful heart and life, He can bring it about. So confess it as the will of God. That is foundational and very essential if we really are believing Him for change.

5. AVOID CONVENIENT REMINDERS.

Since outward stimuli serve as bridgeheads to sin, we need to avoid those reminders. The Bible makes this clear when it says, "Abstain from every form of evil (I Thess. 5:22). We have an obligation to keep our eyes and minds off those things that trigger lust. David fell because of the progression (regression) of events. In II Samuel 11, the account tells us that concerning Bathsheba, David saw, he sent, and he sinned. There was certainly no sin in the first glance. But David didn't confine it to a glance. He stared, he gazed, he concentrated on lust. Then he did the foolish thing, he brought her close to him. He should have run in the opposite direction. Then, of course, this led to sexual sin, fornication and adultery. Then, as usual, the whole thing had to be covered, so he lied and murdered. He got into a hole deeper and deeper. The result was tragic. I think the Bible is so practical. That story was written for us. If stealing is your weakness, never go in a store alone. If drinking is your problem, don't drive by the taverns. If lust is your problem, steer clear of those situations where it can be easily triggered. That's old fashioned practical sense.

6. KNOW THE CONSEQUENCES AND CONCLUSION OF LUST.

Deliverance comes easier when we see the consequence. The Bible says:

> Then desire (lust), when it has conceived, gives birth to sin; and sin when it is full grown brings forth death (James 1:15).

The steps of degeneration lead to death . . . separation from God. Something in a person dies when lust is allowed to run rampant. I think if we really know the final step, it is a sufficient warning.

Now, if it all begins in our thinking, our mental pictures, how can we change that? The answer is really the last step in being loosed from lust.

7. EXPERIENCE THE DAILY CLEANSING OF THE MIND.

It is our mind where the battle takes place. Here, we lose or win the battle. Satan desires that our minds make welcome the lewd, the low, and the vulgar. It's no wonder Paul, over and over again, spoke of the mind. He pleads with us, "Have this mind among your-selves . . ." (Phil. 2:5). Again, "Set your mind on things that are above . . ." (Col. 3:2). We are what we think! "As a man thinketh in his heart, so is he (Prov. 23:7, KJV). For the believer, the Bible calls for the cleansing of our minds: ". . . and be renewed in the spirit of your minds . . ." (Eph. 4:23). Paul further states that our new nature is "renewed in knowledge after the image of its creator" (Col. 3:10).

But how does this renewal come? Are we to take out our brains at night, soak them in bleach, and insert them back in our heads the next day? O, how I wish it were that simple!! Neither does the renewing of our mind come from hypnotism. Nor does it come from some mystical meditation that is not of God. Biblical and effective mind renewal comes by getting God's word etched on our minds. There is no other way. Here is where many are deceived, even Christians. Satan cleverly convinces people that there are some quick remedies and short-cuts to curbing lustful appetites, especially lust of the flesh. Make no mistake about it, nothing short of quality time alone, daily in God's Word, will enable us to get victory here. It's no wonder the Psalmist asked and answered this question so decisively.

> How can a young man keep his way pure? By guarding it according to thy Word (Ps. 119:9).

and again;

> I have laid up thy word in my heart that I might not sin against thee (Ps. 119:11).

The older versions said "Thy word have I HID in my heart. . . ." It takes time to hide something. The Hebrew word used here describes a process of depositing, storing, stacking or laying up. It is a process intended to take some time and be done repeatedly. We can't expect abundant victory at the point of lust if there hasn't been abundant digging at the point of the Word of God.

Here's a challenge. Time the minutes it takes in a normal day for you to eat. Even if you are a breakfast skipper, time your lunch and dinner. The average person spends approximately 23 minutes in which he is actually eating (putting food in one's mouth) at those two meals. But don't forget the snacks, the coffee breaks and the munchies you have between meals and before bed. In all, you are looking at about 27-30 minutes your mouth is moving, chewing and digesting physical food. Now, ready for the challenge? Match the time you spend eating physically with eating spiritually. That's why Paul said: "Let the Word of Christ dwell in you richly. . . ." The word "dwell" means to tabernacle, to camp, to set up tent there. Then Paul says, "richly." Popping a verse down with your vitamins in the morning doesn't cut it. God has created you to be victorious over lust, but He has also provided the wherewithal to do it, His Word! Remember, no shortcuts! Get into God's Word and get God's Word into you. I'm not talking about cramming Bible facts, names, dates, places, etc. into your brain, but rather weaving the beautiful principles of God's Word into your daily living. Remember, it's not how much scripture you have, but how much of you the scripture has that really counts. It's not enough to learn it, but do it.

Do you want to be loosed from lust? It's going to take getting in on God's principles which you have just read. Deliverance is there if you want it.

Here's a prayer for cleansing you might want to pray:

LORD, CLEANSE ME! SCRAPE THE BARNACLES OF LUST AND FILTH FROM MY MIND, WASH ME CLEAN OF ALL THE DEBRIS AND FILTH OF A DIRTY WORLD SO THAT MY FELLOWSHIP WITH YOU WILL BE UNSULLIED. AMEN.

Remember, it is he who has clean hands and a pure heart that shall ascend to the hill of the Lord (Ps. 24:4). Claim your deliverance NOW!

7

FREED FROM FEAR

You would never guess by looking at him that Carl was afraid. He worked as a head chef in a large restaurant, was married, living in a moderately priced, but nice home. But inside, Carl lived in a world of fear. His fears, known only to his wife and me, were not always identifiable, but one thing was sure, he was a virtual prisoner. He stopped going places, doing things, he lost interest in his hobby of woodworking. He withdrew from friends, church, and even his wife. Fear had gripped his life like a vice and wouldn't let go. Like many other silent sufferers today, Carl was being oppressed by a spirit of fear, which if left to run its course, would eventually hospitalize him and render him a mental vegetable. He had even begun to stutter. We began the long painful journey of deliverance.

Fear is as old as the first family of the human race. When Adam and Eve fell in the garden from a position of sinlessness, disobeyed God, and transgressed, the scripture says:

And they heard the sound of the Lord God walking in the garden in the cool of the day, and the man and his wife hid themselves from the

49

presence of the Lord God among the trees of the garden. But the Lord God called to the man and said to him, "Where are you?" And he said, "I heard the sound of thee in the garden and I was afraid because I was naked; and I hid myself" (Gen. 3:8-10).

One cause of fear is definitely disobedience to God. It seems to be axiomatic, that the further man sinks in disobedience to God, the more fears he encounters. The Bible "appears" to contradict itself to some. It says on the one hand, "Fear the Lord," and on the other hand, Jesus said over and over, "Fear not. . . ." We must remember when the Bible speaks of our "fearing" the Lord, it's not the kind of fear where we are afraid of God. It is not a command to be scared or frightened. It is a command to hold God in awe. He is a consuming fire, He is just, He is holy, He is pure, and we need to fear Him in the sense of reverence and awe.

We live in a generation of fear. The news media constantly hawks before us its wares of brutalities, war, immorality, and dreaded nuclear attack. If people aren't afraid, one T.V. newscast can do the trick! The list of fears is endless. In fact Webster describes the phobias; beside each phobia is the name of the thing feared:

ACROPHOBIA high places	KINESOPHOBIA movement
AGOROPHOBIA open spaces	LALOPHOBIA speaking
AICHINOPHOBIA sharp objects	MUSOPHOBIA mice
AILUROPHOBIA cats	MYSOPHOBIA contamination
ANDROPHOBIA men	NECROPHOBIA dead bodies
APEIROPHOBIA infinity	NEOPHOBIA new things
ASTRAPHOBIA thunderstorms	NYCTOPHOBIA night
ASTROPHOBIA stars	OPHIDIOPHOBIA reptiles
AUTOPHOBIA being alone	PEDOPHOBIA infants or kids
BALLISTOPHOBIA missiles	PHAGOPHOBIA eating
BATHOPHOBIA depths	PHONOPHOBIA noise
CHIONOPHOBIA snow	PSYCHROPHOBIA cold
CYNOPHOBIA dogs	PYROPHOBIA fire
DEMOPHOBIA crowds	TAPHEPHOBIA buried alive
ERYTHROPHOBIA red	THALASSOPHOBIA ocean or sea
GAMOPHOBIA marriage	THANATOPHOBIA death
GYNOPHOBIA women	TOXICOPHOBIA poison
HAPTEPHOBIA being touched	ZOOPHOBIA animals
HEMOPHOBIA blood	

The list doesn't stop there. People fear being ugly, unliked, taxes, not having enough money to pay bills, cancer, heart disease, auto accidents, tight places, speed, people and crowds, foods, gaining weight, and the list goes on and on.

I once read about a man whose inferiority complex was so bad a team would huddle, he thought they were talking about him! I share this, not to be facetious, but to point up the reality of fear. Fear cripples, renders us unproductive, robs us of creativity and charm in our lives. The American male, despite his macho look and appearance of success is usually a sitting duck for heart problems. The medical profession is tracing the cause of many young Americans' heart problems to fear. The fear of failure is no respecter of age, sex, or economic level. Teenage suicides lead all other suicides, and the cause is peer pressure brought on by inordinate fears . . . fears of not being "cool," fears of not being accepted, not being one of the bunch, not being popular. This fear consumes so thoroughly that many teens see the only face-saving way out is self-destruction.

The irony of it all is that well over 90% of the things people fear never occur. President Roosevelt was right, after all, when he said, "the only thing we have to fear is fear itself." But what causes these fears? Why are countless millions imprisoned by fears?

The ultimate cause of fear is the inability or refusal to believe in a sovereign God. But the surface reasons can be many. Some fears are born out of one's childhood experiences. Some parents, in the name of safety, become overprotective to the point of fostering un-justified fears. A mother who forbids her son to play football in school for fear he will be injured may be instilling in that child in-ordinate fears about physical safety. Other parents are over-indulgent with their children, giving them everything they ask for. Later in life, when they don't get everything, they get an insecure feeling about not having "things" and begin to fear. Still, other parents practice physical violence with their children in the name of raising disciplined children. Over-reacting to misbehavior by abusive and extreme physical beating can create excessive fear of authority figures later on. Sexual abuse as a child can breed a fear very hard to shake later in life. How tragic that so much child molesting is coming to light today. Many are the newlyweds whose marriages are shattered early on because one of the partners had been sexually abused as a child,

51

and now they are terrified about their physical relationship. A workaholic recently confessed to me the reason he devotes 72 hours a week to his job; "It's simple . . . I was raised in abject poverty . . . my father never had one nickel to spare, and we children often did without the bare necessities. I vowed my family would never suffer that way." This man, by confession, lives a fear dominated life . . . scared to death that he won't make enough to have enough! Lack of faith, then, becomes the root of all fear—lack of faith in the sovereignty of a loving and providential God.

Someone left a motto on my desk once. It simply read: "FEAR KNOCKED, FAITH ANSWERED, NO ONE WAS THERE!" It's true, the iceblock of fear quickly melts with burning faith. So many Christians today labor under the unresolved guilt syndrome. God has forgiven their past sins, no matter how horrible they are, yet they cringe with fear daily that they aren't doing enough to merit that kind of grace. We forget that grace is dispensed without the aid of merit, or works, or deeds, or acts of penance. Accepting our acceptance becomes the challenge. I once read about a man who told his pastor that he couldn't sleep because he was afraid. Further into the conversation, his pastor discovered that the man had committed a terrible sin after he became a Christian. "And did you confess that sin to God?" "Confess it?" retorted the man, "I confessed it a thousand times!" The pastor replied, "That's 999 times too many. You should have confessed it once, then thanked him 999 times!" Our failure to believe in a loving, forgiving God is contagious. It also causes us not to believe in the God of protection, the God of supply, the God of faithfulness, the God of healing, or the God of power.

A little boy was asked by his mother to get her broom, which was out on the back porch. That porch was dark, and he couldn't reach the light switch. "I'm scared, Mommy, to go out there, it's dark!" the boy said to his mother. The mother, desiring to teach him a good Bible lesson, said, "Oh, don't worry, son, the Lord is out there!" The boy said, "Then Lord, would you please hand me that broom?" Some might interpret that as cowardice, but I see it as wisdom. We need to call on the name of the Lord right in the midst of our fears. The Psalmist said:

> Even though I walk through the valley of the shadow of death, I will fear no evil . . . (Ps. 23:4).

How could the Psalmist say that? Weren't there evils all about in a shepherd's life? Weren't there crags, wild animals, serpents, and the elements of the night threatened? Yes, the evils were there, but he feared no evil, "FOR THOU ART WITH ME!" Presence doesn't make the difference. Faith in the presence does!

Sometimes, the answer to the very thing we fear the most is so close, we miss it. Who hasn't searched and searched for their car keys? Not under the mat on the floor, not in any of our pockets or purses, not above the visor . . . we're ready to panic. Glancing at the ignition, there they are, IN THE CAR! Of all places for keys to be!

An old story is worth retelling. A party of shipwrecked sailors were drifting in an open boat on the Atlantic ocean. They had no water, and were suffering agonies from thirst. Another small boat came within hailing distance, and when the shipwrecked mariners cried out for water, the newcomers said, "Let down your bucket." This sounded like cruel mockery. But when the advice was repeated several times, one of the sailors dipped the bucket overboard—and drew up clean, fresh, sparkling water! For several days they had been sailing through fresh water and did not know it. They were out of sight of land, but off the estuary of the Amazon which carries fresh water out to sea many miles. Like the sailors, we simply need to let our buckets down.

At other times, the very thing we fear is the blessing in disguise, and is, in fact, the answer to our fears. Once when the disciples were on the lake in the midst of a hurricane-force storm, Jesus came to them, walking on the water. Listen to the account:

> And he saw that they were making headway painfully, for the wind was against them. And about the fourth watch of the night, he came to them walking on the sea. He meant to pass by them, but when they saw him walking on the sea, they thought it was a ghost and cried out; for they all saw him, and were terrified. But immediately he spoke to them and said "Take heart, it is I; have no fear." And he got into the boat with them and the wind ceased, and they were utterly astounded (Mark 6:48-51).

Imagine! What they thought was a ghost turned out to be Jesus, whose presence in their boat calmed their fears. He commanded them to have no fear. That means that there are some things in life we are not to fear at all. Some fear, of course, is good. We call it "healthy respect." We "respect" a hot stove, a poisonous snake, the undertow of an ocean, or a sharp knife. But God doesn't want His people living in fear of anything.

Here are 4 proven steps, when taken, that will free you from fear.

1. First, ask, IS WHAT I FEAR BIGGER THAN GOD? Without knowing what your fear is, I can answer that question for you, NO! I have a small sign behind my desk chair, high where all can see. It reads, "GOD IS GREATER THAN ANY PROBLEM I HAVE." I like that. I glance at it several times a day. It helps put everything in perspective.

2. FACE FEAR AND CALL IT WHAT IT IS, SIN! Ask yourself, "What did Jesus command us to fear?" The answer to that is nothing! In fact, he said just the opposite; "Have no fear. . . ." To continue to fear is to be blatantly disobedient to God.

3. Next, ask, DOES WHAT I FEAR HAVE A TRACK RECORD OF HARMING ME IN THE PAST? The usual answer to that is no. Since 99% of those things we fear never occur, we need to face them only as a mirage to deceive us.

4. REBUKE THE SPIRIT OF FEAR IN THE NAME OF JESUS CHRIST. Yes, you have that authority. Since fear is from the devil, of the devil, by the devil and for the devil, we need to speak authoritatively to that attitude, and mean it when we speak it. Once done, then live the life that matches your talk. Satan works best through fearful, beaten down people. If you don't want to be an effective challenge for his cause and his purpose, then be free from fear, NOW!

When you let Jesus in your boat, the storm ceases, and the fears are gone. The ultimate answer to fear is accepting, knowing, and honoring Jesus Christ as Lord of your life.

Carl found that secret and was delivered from all his fears. You can too!

8

ARRESTING YOUR ANGER

Years ago, a business man traveling by train was careful to make arrangements for his sure departure at the right stop. He told the conductor upon boarding, that he had to get off the train in Chicago for a very important business meeting. He warned the conductor that he was a very heavy sleeper, and that the conductor might have to bodily put him off if he had trouble getting him awake. The train was well past Chicago when early morning arrived and the man awoke in his berth, looked at his watch, came down, contacted the conductor, and really gave him a piece of his mind. In anger, he got off at the next stop. Another conductor who witnessed the whole incident, said to the conductor, "Boy, was that man ever mad." "If you think he's mad," said the conductor, "you should have seen the man I awoke and put off in Chicago!"

We live in a world of anger! Law enforcement agencies are telling us that anger and violence are up appreciably, especially in the home. Reports of wife abuse, child abuse, and violence in general abound. It has become so volatile that in many states laws have recently been changed to allow law enforcement officials to enter domestic violence situations and make arrests. The home, long protected from police surveillance, has become so violent and out of control that new laws are now demanded.

In the state of Washington a man pulled a gun on another man outside the theater where both had seen a movie of violence. After a brief argument he shot and killed the man and his brother.

Sociologists today are saying that this generation will be remembered in history as the generation of violence. Of course, anger is a spiritual problem. Behind every act of physical violence is a person whose thought processes have been triggered to retaliate with a view to harm.

Some people spend a lifetime bound by anger. For some, the pattern began as a child where anger was used to get one's way. For others, it was learned from parents whose lifestyle in and out of the home was one of incessant anger. A young man in his early twenties recently said to me, "I never remember a time when my father wasn't angry about something."

Biblically, anger began early: "So Cain was very angry, and his countenance fell" (Gen. 4:5b). The rest of it is history. He killed his blood brother Abel just because Abel's offering was accepted and Cain's wasn't!

Esau hated Jacob because Jacob stole the blessing. He vowed to kill his brother (Gen. 27:41). Moses became enraged when he looked on the oppression of his own people. One day when he saw an Egyptian beating a Hebrew, in a fit of rage he killed him and hid the body. Saul became exceedingly angry with his own son Jonathan and David. His jealousy and anger against David almost drove him mad.

The list of things that drives people to anger is endless. JEALOUSY: A jealous spirit brings anger out faster than anything I know. Jealousy over someone else's clothes, promotion, looks, new car, etc. can trigger an angry spirit. Much marital conflict can be traced to anger caused by an overprotective spouse. Even among Christian people, jealousies develop. "He got the solo part and I didn't!" "She was made chairman and I wasn't!" "They got elected and I didn't!" And so it goes. . . . COVETOUSNESS: Someone has called coveting "adoring and desiring the unpossessed." Violence often follows an unfulfilled covet. The Bible says:

> You desire and do not have, so you kill. And you covet and cannot obtain so you fight and wage war . . . (James 4:2a).

Anger is often born of a covetous spirit. OFFENSES: Offended people usually strike back by anger. I saw it happen in the Seattle airport. A man was bumped from a flight. His seat had been taken by another due to computer foul-up. He became out of control. He had to be bodily removed from the aircraft. He threatened lawsuits and yelled obscenities against the airlines. To be sure, he had been wronged, and wrongfully wronged! But his anger only intensified the situation. It solved nothing. He really needed to hear the verse, "Vengeance is mine, I will repay, says the Lord" (Rom. 12:19).

It is amazing how the actions of others can control our tempers and cause us to react in a way we always later regret. We need to stop and realize the liabilities of our angry spirits. Anger, uncontrolled, unharnessed, and unleashed, has physical effects. Blood pressure almost always goes up. The digestive and emotional system temporarily closes down. Concentration goes out the window. Good judgment no longer prevails. Anger reduces most of its victims to little people who say things they can never retrieve . . . things they deeply regret at some point later in life.

Not all anger expresses itself overtly. The slow, seething kind of anger that is held inside is usually the most destructive kind. This is the anger that never strikes with the fist or the tongue, but expresses itself just as effectively by the silent treatment toward others.

Maybe you are a victim of anger. Maybe its ugly tentacles have wrapped themselves around your life to restrict and reduce you. What is the answer? Here are some very simple steps, when taken, that will truly arrest your anger.

1. REMEMBER WHAT ANGER WILL NOT DO. The Bible says:

> . . . be slow to anger, for the anger of man does not work the righteousness of God (James 1:19b-20).

Anger contributes nothing at all to the working out of God's plan in your life or anyone else's life. If vengeance belongs to God, then He is the chairman of the "getting back" committee, not you.

Anger can't right a wrong, preserve a friendship, build character, even the score, or assist the Lord in any way. It will never bring peace, heal a rift, or correct an erroneous situation. It only intimidates others and brings out the worst in everyone.

2. LET ANGER DIE DAILY! The Bible says:

> Be angry, but do not sin. Do not let the sun go down on your anger (Eph. 4:26).

o

Like dirt on the body, anger needs to be washed off daily. Many have misunderstood the above scripture by mistakenly taking the first part, "Be angry . . ." as a command. It is not a command to obey, but a condition to control! (i.e. Even if you find yourself in a state of anger, don't ever go to bed with it.) At the close of each day, anger doesn't need to be filed for future reference. It needs to be flung away for the sake of future sanity. By the way, a good rule for you who are married, NEVER go to sleep at night if the two of you are angry with each other. In whatever state you go to sleep, you awaken, even though it may be filed in your self-conscious. In whatever state of mind we retire, sleep has a way of congealing our attitudes. The phrase, "I'll sleep on it" does not apply to angry attitudes.

3. REMEMBER, ANGER'S STAR VICTIM IS YOU! The Bible says:

> A fool gives full vent his anger, but a wise man quietly holds it back (Prov. 29:11).

Anger, unleashed, unbridled, and let go makes such a fool of us. Its intent is to do harm to others, but the truth is, we are the losers, not they. The minute I begin hating another and seek to do them harm, I become their slave. It is they who are controlling me, not the other way around. Anger makes me the victim, not the victor.

Larry was seething when he came into my office. In good faith he had loaned a close friend some money. The friend had skipped town, left no forwarding address, and no tangible clue as to his whereabouts. "Boy, when I do get a hold of him, he'll wish he had never met me!" Those were Larry's words. His "friend" had him . . . as a pawn in the palm of his hand. Since there was nothing anyone could do at this time, my advice was to commit both Larry and the unpaid money to the Lord. I counseled Larry to pray that his "friend" would feel a burden for the obligation from the Lord and repay the debt, thus salvaging the friendship. Though it was hard, Larry, because he was a Christian, agreed to pursue that route. Within only a matter of weeks, Larry received a check from his friend with a note of apology.

It was truly providential the friend left town or a good friendship would have been broken, the money probably not repaid, and bitterness on the part of the two men would have eaten them alive.

4. Finally, SOME ANGER CANNOT BE REDEEMED! That is not to say that God does not forgive our anger, but though forgiven, indelible scars remain on us and other people all their life. There is a man in Texas confined to a wheelchair, because in a fit of rage and anger, he fell down a flight of stairs doing permanent damage to his spine. Anger costs, too. A few years ago, a human interest story told of a man who had been stopped for easing through a stop sign. Because few things had gone right for him that day, he bolted out of the car, and began to be verbally abusive to the officer. Before the entire incident was over, he was given citations for abusive speech, resisting arrest, speeding, leaving the scene of an offense, and operating a vehicle with an expired license! His fines exceeded $1000, to say nothing of a ruined driving record. To top it all off, the officer had only intended to reprimand him in the initial stop and let him go! O, the price of anger.

The basic, root cause of all anger is selfishness. Although we have become experts in rationalizing our behavior, people get angry because they become selfish. Anger always comes when someone has "violated" my rights. We often excuse our anger by prefacing our remarks with . . . "Well, you would be angry too if. . . ." Our case is always different. Our situation is always the exception. The truth is, anger is inexcusable for the Christian, especially when God has provided a way for us to be free from anger.

Jesus gave us the best antidote for anger. In the sermon on the mount, Jesus said:

> To him who strikes you on the cheek, offer the other also, and from him who takes away your coat, do not withhold even your shirt (Luke 6:29).

There is a principle here which will work when tried. It is the principle of returning what is never expected. When someone backs into your new car of only 3 days, how do you respond? If your child spills ink on your brand new carpet, how do you respond? Soft answers still turn away wrath. The next time you are yelled at, even if unjustly, respond tenderly with an apology. Your offender will be melted and stripped of his anger, and you will have averted your own. Have you noticed how quickly an argument stops between two people when one shuts up? It's amazing.

The next time you are ready for a case of the "angries," just offer it to God and say, "Lord, this is your problem, you handle it, and I'll stay out of it." You will end up the victor, and, by the way, God will handle it the way it's supposed to be handled!

Humbly pray this: "LORD, MELT MY ANGER, STRIP ME OF VENGEANCE, TAKE AWAY FROM ME ALL THOUGHTS OF RETALIATION AND GETTING 'EVEN.' ENABLE ME TO RESPOND TO MY ENEMIES WITH LOVE AND HUMILITY UNTIL THEY CEASE TO BE MY ENEMIES. AMEN."

9

GO GUILT, GO!

He tried nervously to talk of trivial things. I knew our lunch together was hard for him. I was the last person he ever wanted to talk to, but yet the first person he called to help him out of the morass of his guilt. I was determined not to "pull" it out of him, so I listened to small talk, until finally, after the waitress brought our food, he blurted out with a shower of tears, "I can't hold it in any longer!" So along with my reuben and fries, came the saddest admission I had ever heard. At 42, Tom had gone through what so many needlessly face. I call it the Forties Fiasco. A man is more than halfway through his working life. He's been married an average of 20 years. Then it hits . . . a restlessness with questions. "Have I really done what I'm capable of doing? Is there something I missed? Did I marry the wrong woman? With gray appearing around my temples, am I losing my attractiveness to other women? Am I fulfilled?" In this unplanned sea of doubts, the "affair" begins quite innocently at first. The computer programmer, who is having severe problems with her husband, seems to understand. She smiles at him. She brings him coffee, and soon it's lunch, then a drink after work, and then the inevitable occurs, a full-blown affair is under way.

Tom's was a classic example. It happened just that way. It had been in progress for almost a year. He lived a lie before his wife for one year now. He had lived a lie before his two children for a year. He could hold it in no longer. Like a boil that festers and begins to be infected, Tom's poisonous sin had to be lanced. Painful? Yes, but necessary. Timing? Poor, but no more time-outs. The guilt had done its work. The sin confessed, the burden lifted . . . partially. How would he tell his wife? Who else should know? How was he to break it off? What would he say? We worked it all through, the sin was confessed to the appropriate people, healing set in, and Tom's marriage and family are on the mend. Only one lingering, pesty symptom was left. HOW DO YOU ACCEPT GOD'S ACCEPTANCE? HOW DO YOU ACCEPT FORGIVENESS?

Many today who wear the name of Christ live in constant fear of being zapped by God's spanking hand when they sin. They have little sense of their security and their position in Christ.

Guilt is a marvelous device God has created to drive us to Himself. But once we have reached our destination (God), to continue to hold on to that guilt is a denial of God's redemptive process that makes us whole. Guilt is like the temperature gauge on our car. The light comes on to say our engine is overheating. Our problem isn't the light, but the engine. Our job is not to get the light off, but the engine corrected. By the same token, guilt is God's great built-in indicator in our spirits that an alien (Satan) is overheating and hurting our spirits. When we go along with the attack, a good case of guilt surfaces, and until it is properly dealt with, it's like the rain in the Pacific Northwest: IT WON'T GO AWAY!

The Bible makes it very clear, that as believers, Spirit filled, God-fearing, Bible-loving, blood-washed Christians, we HAVE forgiveness in Christ.

In Him we have redemption, the forgiveness of our trespasses, according to the riches of His grace, which He lavished upon us (Eph. 1:7).

So many true believers are suffering today from a pseudo-guilt. God never meant us to bear guilt once it has been absolved. There is an identity crisis today among Christians with which Satan has a heyday.

They don't know who they are. As in Tom's case, confession of sin is made to God and the appropriate people, forgiveness is extended by God, but accepting the acceptance becomes the hang-up. First of all, let it be clear. When we are saved, we are washed and cleansed not only from the power of sin, but from the guilt of sin. The Bible says again:

> If we walk in the light as He is in the light, we have fellowship with one another, and the blood of Jesus His Son, cleanses us from all sin (I John 1:7).

Notice what John said, he said from ALL SIN. A-L-L sin! That's past, present, and future. That's every kind and strain of sin. That's every volume of sin, either a quart, or sixty million gallons. Because those He saves He keeps, we have every reason to affirm and reaffirm our security in Christ. The scripture is replete with promises, assuring us of the certainty and sureness of our salvation. Jesus said:

> My sheep hear by voice, and I know them, and they follow me, and I give them eternal life, and they shall never perish, and no one shall snatch them out of my hand (John 10:27-28).

That's the Lord's personal commitment to every true believer.

Somewhere along the line, people developed a system that said it was His grace that got us in, but it is our works and performance that keeps us in. Of course, that is contrary to scripture. Our works and performance are done BECAUSE we are in, not in order to GET IN OR STAY IN! If His grace was strong enough to get us in while we were enemies and rebellious, isn't His grace strong enough to keep us in now that we are His friends? Paul really settled this issue in Romans 5. He said:

> For if while we were enemies we were reconciled to God by the death of His Son, much more now that we are reconciled shall we be saved by His life (Rom. 5:10).

If the greater is true, the lesser is true! If this is true, (and it is) what does that do with our guilt? God says it's gone. For us to say it's still there when God declares it's gone is to make ourselves greater than God.

But what about the guilt we get as believers because of the lingering sins we commit on a daily basis? That guilt also is meant to drive us to God, to confess the sin, NOT TO REGAIN OUR POSITION OF SALVATION, but to get our fellowship with the Lord back where it ought to be. Sin for a believer damages his fellowship, not his relationship. My son is biologically mine. His mother and I are blood parents. He may go against my will sometimes, do things that disappoint me or damage my character, but this does not revoke his sonship. His fellowship with me may be strained or even temporarily severed at times, but his relationship with me is intact. Likewise, the Father who adopted us is not eager to expel us from His family. Only our own willful rejection of our covenant relationship with Christ could cause God to reject us. Nothing else—no external power— can ever separate us from the love of Christ!

So, we need to hear again, and again, OUR POSITION IN CHRIST IS A SECURE ONE. That's why the Bible says:

> I write this to you who believe in the name of the Son of God that you may know that you have eternal life (I John 5:13).

Then why do Christians continue to be slaves of guilt? Why do they continue to cringe before a merciful God? Why is the joy gone from their life? Is it because they live in a relationship to God of fear and insecurity? The answer, of course, is that they have failed to appropriate what is theirs.

5 Steps To Rid Your Life of Guilt as a Believer

1. TRUST THE WORD OF GOD, NOT YOUR FEELINGS. We have come to base so much on feelings. Feelings are fickle. They come, they go. Regardless of how you feel, don't pin your faith and hope on feelings. Pin your hope on the surety of God's Word. If the Bible says you are clean before God because of Christ's righteousness, then YOU ARE CLEAN!

2. RE-AFFIRM DAILY WHO YOU ARE IN CHRIST! You are a blood-washed child of God. You belong to the Father by right of creation and purchase. I've found it helpful to simply say daily: "I'M YOUR CHILD GOD, AND THUS I HAVE NO REASON TO FEEL OR EXPERIENCE GUILT TODAY."

3. REMEMBER, THE HOLY SPIRIT TESTIFIES ABOUT YOUR POSITION TOO! The Bible says in Romans 8:16, "It is the Spirit Himself bearing witness with our spirit, that we are children of God. . . ."

Remember, we have no right to say to the Holy Spirit, "O Sir, you must be mistaken, today I'm not a child of God, because I slipped up and sinned." Don't fuss with the Holy Spirit. If He bears witness to our position, believe Him. He's right!

4. REMEMBER, YOU HAVE AN INHERITANCE THAT IS SURE! That ought to be a big motivator that keeps you from living in a state of guilt. Again, in Romans 8:16, Paul said, ". . . AND IF CHILDREN, then heirs, heirs of God, and fellow heirs with Christ. . . ." But, you may be saying, "Is that inheritance still intact if I sin?" Well, let's let God answer that question; notice how Peter recorded the words of the Holy Spirit:

> Blessed be the God and Father of our Lord, Jesus Christ! By His great mercy we have been born anew to a living hope through the resurrection of Jesus Christ from the dead, and TO AN INHERITANCE WHICH IS IMPERISHABLE, UNDEFILED, AND UNFADING, KEPT IN HEAVEN FOR YOU, WHO BY GOD'S POWER ARE GUARDED THROUGH FAITH FOR A SALVATION READY TO BE REVEALED IN THE LAST TIME (I Peter 1:3-5).

Wow! Those verses are loaded with power. First, the inheritance that is ours is imperishable. That means it can't be destroyed. It is totally indestructible. Secondly, it is undefiled. Nothing can pollute it, dilute it, poison it, or make it unclean in any way. Thirdly, it is unfading. It won't tarnish with time or wear. It is unchangeable and unalterable. Then, Peter says an amazing thing we usually miss. He says in verse 5 that we are guarded by God's power! Notice, we are not guarded by our faithfulness, not our cleverness, nor our strength, but by God's power. How exciting, God has not only preserved the inheritance, He is preserving the INHERITORS! That's you and me.

5. REMEMBER SATAN'S DESIRE FOR YOU! What is it? Satan desires, even more than your demise, to render you ineffective, unproductive, unfruitful, a living example of contradiction. What is the BEST way to pull that off? It's simple. When all else fails, Satan wants you to feel unworthy, guilt-ridden, and in bondage. He could really fulfill his plan in your life if he can get you on a perpetual guilt trip. Unfortunately, too many believers today walk and talk without a boldness and confidence about their security in Christ. Satan has done his usual number on them. What is the greatest antidote for this? You need to take authority and let Satan KNOW you

have authority, and in the name of Jesus Christ, call him off your case. How do you do this? Maybe this special delivery message to Satan from you will do it. At any rate, read on, and believe what you read. He'll get the general idea!

SATAN, TAKE NOTE AND LISTEN WELL. YOU WILL NOT CONQUER ME. I'M BLOOD WASHED, DAILY DELIVERED, STRONGLY SANCTIFIED, SPIRIT SOAKED AND WORD INDWELT, YOU ARE WASTING YOUR ENERGY ON ME. I HAVE SET MY FACE, I'M LINKED WITH SOVEREIGN AND ETERNAL POWER. YOU'RE A DECEIVER, BUT YOU WON'T DECEIVE ME. YOU'RE A ROARING LION, BUT I'M NOT DEVOURABLE. YOU'RE EXTREMELY SUBTLE, BUT I'M ON TO YOUR WAYS. YOU PARADE AS AN ANGEL OF LIGHT, BUT I WALK IN A STRONGER LIGHT. YOUR DAYS OF DECEPTION ARE OVER WITH ME. I WON'T BE DETOURED, DERAILED, DISTRACTED, DISTORTED, DISCOURAGED, OR DISILLUSIONED BY YOUR SCHEMES. YOUR INFLUENCE WILL NOT CROSS THE NO TRESPASSING SIGN ON THE GATE OF MY LIFE. I'M OFF LIMITS TO YOU NOW. MY DOORS ARE CLOSED TO YOU. YOU WON'T WALK IN, CRAWL IN, SLITHER IN, SNEAK IN, PRY IN, OR BARGE INTO MY LIFE. I HAVE A PERMANENT GUEST NOW THAT LIVES INSIDE, AND HE CANNOT SHARE MY TEMPLE WITH YOU. YOU MAY LURE, LIE, LINGER, LURCH, LAUGH, BUT YOU WON'T COME IN. YOUR DAYS ARE NUMBERED, YOUR KINGDOM DOOMED, YOUR DESIGNS ARE DWINDLING, YOUR EVIL ERODING, YOUR DEVILISHNESS DISSOLVING, YOUR DESIGNS DECAYING, YOUR PROGRESS IS POISONED, AND YOUR ULTIMATE VICTORY HAS BEEN CANCELED. YOU CAN'T TRAP ME WITH YOUR TEASING, SOIL ME WITH YOUR SUBTLEY, OR DEFEAT ME WITH YOUR DECEPTION. HE THAT IS IN ME IS GREATER THAN YOU. SO GET OFF MY PROPERTY, THE DAY OF YOUR FINAL BIDDING IS NOT FAR AWAY.

Remember, "There is therefore now no condemnation for those who are in Christ Jesus" (Rom. 8:1). Want to know who "those" are? That's you, if you're a Christian! You can believe it . . . God's Word said it!

10

GOOD GRIEF

"I can't, I can't, I just can't go on, the loss is too much!" She was incredibly weak from crying. She had cried without any sleep for nearly 14 hours. Her young husband, with two of his buddies, had started up to Canada in good weather in a friend's 4-place plane. They had not counted on the excessive wind drafts whirling through the Cascade mountains. The plane was found only about forty feet from the peak, where it had slammed into a solid rock wall. All three men were instantly killed. The young widow's hopes and dreams were shattered by one phone call. It was my job to offer comfort and hope. She dwelt on the word loss. The dictionary defines grief in these words: "Deep sorrow or mental distress caused by loss, remorse, affliction, etc." Loss always brings a form of grief. It may be the loss of a loved one, the loss of a job, the loss of a family member to drugs, the loss of a friend who has moved away, the loss of health, or the loss of a mate in separation or divorce. There are several truths we must remember in dealing with grief. These truths will enable you to face your grief, then be victorious over it.

1. SOME GRIEF IS NORMAL AND SHOULDN'T BE FEARED

It's normal to experience sorrow when a loved one is taken in death. Though we who believe in spiritual metamorphosis do not grieve "as others do who have no hope" (I Thess. 4:13), separation brings grief. I wept when I received the news by phone that my father had died. Though I had been separated from him by miles for years, he was still my father. I immediately began to think of all the childhood memories in which he played a major role. I knew I would never see his living face again here on earth. That brought sorrow. I sat in a waiting room at 4 AM and cried when my assistant pastor in Oklahoma slipped into eternity after his cancer choked him to death. Again, all the memories came flooding into my mind . . . memories of times we labored together, laughed together, and prayed together. To hear news like that and go on as though nothing has occurred is hypocrisy. There is no room for being "macho" when death comes to separate loved ones from us. It's all right to cry, and that initial grief work is not only natural, but essential for later weeks and months.

2. SOME GRIEF IS PUBLIC AND SOME IS PRIVATE

There is a therapy in crying in the arms of a friend, wife, husband, parent, or child. Sorrow shared has a binding effect not experienced anyplace else. But there is part of our grief that must be done in private, with no one but us and God. It's not that we are ashamed that someone will find us crying, it's just that a certain percentage of grief needs to be experienced in the privacy of the prayer closet. Sometimes we need to be alone, not because we are morose and too serious, but because some things are best settled that way.

3. EXTENDED GRIEF IS UNWHOLESOME AND UNNATURAL

Three to five months is a fairly normal grieving period after the death of a very close loved one. Grief extended beyond that time can be destructive and affect virtually every part of our life. The Psalmist said, "Weeping may tarry for the night, but joy comes in the morning" (Ps. 30:5). What a promise! The young widow asked me that day, "Will the pain of my grief EVER go away?" I assured her it would. It did. Those who entertain grief as a guest on a very extended visit court problems greater than grief. First of all, the deceased would not want us to go into a permanent shell and hide forever behind the twin masks of depression and grief. Secondly, we need to get on with life, not only for our own sake, but for the sake of those about us. Life goes on, with or without us on board. I saw a desk sign that read: "TOMORROW HAS BEEN CANCELLED DUE TO LACK OF ENERGY." It may well have read, ". . . DUE TO LACK OF JOY, DESIRE, MOTIVATION, OR WHATEVER." To harbor grief not only brings misery down on us, but to all about us. It isn't fair to the deceased, to our peers, or to us. Some find a morbid consolation in holding on to the possessions of the deceased. It's almost like, "If I can't have him, I can have whatever he left as a reminder." Of course, no one would suggest that you discard all of your loved one's possessions the day after the funeral. But to hold on for months and years, and relive the death over and over is counter-productive to normal healing and restoration. Such retention fosters a pre-occupation with morbidity that is unwholesome for all concerned.

Then, how can grief be transformed into serenity and biblical joy?

First, REMEMBER, OTHERS HAVE SUFFERED GRIEF AS WELL AS YOU. You are not alone in walking through the valley of shadows. You are not the first to cry a river of tears. Welcome to the fellowship of the sorrowful! Even Jesus went through that valley. He wept at the tomb of Lazarus. He wept over a dense and rejecting city. He wept in the Garden of Gethsemane when he realized he was going to die. He was a "man of sorrows, and acquainted with grief." He is able to minister to you in your grief, because He's been there.

> For we have not a high priest who is unable to sympathize with our weaknesses, but one who in every respect has been tempted as we are, yet without sin (Heb. 4:15).

Secondly, GRIEF PROPERLY HANDLED STRENGTHENS YOUR FIBRE.

Robert B. Hamilton said it best:

> I walked a mile with Pleasure,
> She chattered all the way,
> But left me none the wiser,
> For all she had to say.
>
> I walked a mile with Sorrow,
> And ne'er a word said she;
> But, oh, the things I learned from her,
> When Sorrow walked with me!

Grief is like boiling water. You drop an egg into boiling water, and it will harden. Drop a potato in that same water, and it becomes soft and edible. Some people are hardened by grief; others are tempered and softened.

I stood by the bedside of a five-year-old who had brought such joy to his young parents. I saw what was left after leukemia had ravaged that youngster. In the last days his only response would come when his mother would lay her hand on his fevered brow and quote scripture after scripture. Late one evening, while his parents hovered over his bed, he went to be with Jesus forever. After the tears, the grief, the sadness, I saw a ministry begin. I saw that mother and father begin to minister as only they could to other parents who would face the same grim reality. When we are thrown the dagger of grief, we can catch it by the blade and be cut, or we can catch it by the handle and use it for our good. It's up to us!

Years ago, I read about an old German legend which told of a man who built his castle on the Rhine. From crag to crag and turret to turret he hung wires, hoping that the winds as they blew upon this great Aeolian harp, might make sweet music. Long and patiently he waited, and round his castle winds from the four corners of heaven blew, and still no music came. But one night, there arose a huricane tossing the Rhine to fury; the black sky was stabbed with lightning and the thunder rolled, the earth trembled, and the winds were shrieking. The Baron went to his castle door to view the terrifying scene . . . when Hark! The sound of music like angels singing through the storm and suddenly, the Baron realized what had happened. His harp, strung from crag to crag, had come to life at last. The tempest had given it a soul. That oft-told tale goes down to the heart of life's deep mystery, how often it is only when trouble comes, that a man's true quality stands revealed.

Sorrow has an amazing capacity to bring out in us and from us a quality of sensitivity and an ability to help others we would never otherwise have. When the winds of sorrow blow, we can allow them to topple us, or play the most beautiful music through us ever played. Tears have a way of washing unwelcome debris from our lives. To escape the natural work of grief is to deprive God the opportunity to do just that.

There is another principle we often overlook about grief. YOUR SORROW IS NEVER OVERLOOKED BY GOD! The Psalmist said an amazing thing about God concerning grief and sorrow:

> Thou hast kept count of my tossings; put my tears in thy bottle . . . !
> Are they not in thy book? This I know, that God is for me (Ps. 56:8, 9b).

I especially like the part where it says that God has put my tears in His bottle. Not one is wasted or shed unnoticed. God is aware. He must have many bottles, for there is so much grief in this world. He gathers up our grief, and files it away. What a promise!!

One cannot but be moved by the story of Jesus walking into the city of Nain. When Luke records this incident, he makes sure to mention some pertinent facts. He says that as Jesus neared the city, he spotted a funeral procession. The corpse was a man, but not just any man. This man was the only son of his mother. That statement is especially significant for two reasons. First, for a Jewish woman to be sonless was tantamount to shame. Secondly, this young man was probably her only hope of livelihood. The woman was in deep sorrow and weeping. Jesus was moved by the scene, and he acted. He spoke to the youth saying, "Young man, I say to you, Arise" (Luke 7:14). But the most tender moment comes when the account says; "And the dead man sat up, and began to speak, AND HE GAVE HIM TO HIS MOTHER" (emphasis mine) (Luke 7:15). He gave him to his mother. Jesus restored what death had stolen, the presence of a son, a breadwinner, a loved one. Here is miraculous intervention on the part of the Son of God, NOT just for the purpose of displaying his power, but because He was greatly moved by the intense grief of a widowed mother. No, your grief will never go unnoticed by the Lord, no matter how deep and real it is to you.

Paul broke out in praise to God for the sake of the Corinthian believers when he wrote:

> Blessed be the God and Father of our Lord Jesus Christ, the father
> of mercies, and the God of all comfort, who comforts us in all our
> afflictions . . ." (II Cor. 1:3, 4b).

David knew what sorrow was. I'm sure that in his perennial retreat from King Saul, there were many sleepless, lonely nights he sat in the woods, crying and seeking the face of God. It must have seemed to him more than once that nobody cared. It's no wonder tears had been his food day and night. Thus, when he writes what he did, he wrote out of personal experiences. From those experiences, he could say:

The Lord is near to the broken-hearted and saves the crushed in spirit (Ps. 34:18).

What a statement! What a promise! The next verse is even more victorious!

Many are the afflictions of the righteous; But the Lord delivers them out of them all (Ps. 34:19).

God has promised to deliver us from our grief. That deliverance always comes at His impeccable timing, not ours.

Yet another principle about grief we need to remember is this: YOU NEED TO COOPERATE WITH GOD TO RETURN YOUR LIFE TO JOY AND PRODUCTIVITY. Again, King David was a good example. When he received word that his son Absalom was dead, he went into his chamber and wept his heart out. The Bible says that his sorrow was contagious; "So the victory that day was turned into mourning for all the people; for the people heard that day, 'The King is grieving for his son'" (II Sam. 19:2). You may recall, it was Joab who came to David and encouraged him to stop brooding over his deep sorrow. It was evident that David could not be an effective, successful leader and king as long as he was locked up in his room crying day and night. After Joab's visit, David came out of his chamber. The account says, "Then the king arose and took his seat in the gate, and they were all told, 'Behold, the king is sitting in the gate'; and all the people came before the king." The grief was over, and David returned to leadership and productivity. It didn't mean that he didn't hurt at times, but there is a time when we need to cooperate with God, and get on with our lives after a grieving experience.

Maybe now you are asking, "But how can I be delivered from the valley of grief?" I believe there are 4 steps we need to take.

STEP 1: RECOGNIZE THE STAGES OF GRIEF

Grief goes through at least three different stages. In them all, grief needs to be properly expressed. The first stage is the crisis or critical stage. In the case of death, this stage usually lasts up through the funeral. At first there is shock, surprise, like the blow of a hammer.

"My loved one is dead!" There may even be a hint of denial when you first hear the news. A numbness sets in, and we can't believe what is happening. It's here of course, that friends are so important. It's not what they say, but the fact they are there. This is not a time for friends to give pious reasons for why it happened, or to project theological reasons for it all. The need is for a loving arm and a listening ear. Words really aren't very necessary at this stage. The second stage of grief is what I call the reality stage. It usually lasts for 7 to 10 weeks. It is during this time the bereaved deals with the fact their loved one is gone, and won't be coming back in the flesh. This is often a time of loneliness. The multitude of friends that were there for a few days or weeks after you lost your loved one are now gone. A few may call, but that soon stops. Finally, there is the building stage. It's here you build new structures, maybe make a new set of friends, and re-establish communication with the old ones. It's at the beginning of this stage the bereaved really gets the feeling that life is worth going on, and that there are some joys ahead. So, recognize the stages of grief. The time span may change a bit, but you must go through those stages.

STEP 2: GET INTO GOD'S WORD LIKE YOU NEVER HAVE!

Nothing, I repeat, NOTHING, brings deliverance from grief more thoroughly than etching God's word on your mind in large doses. Determine to read the Bible through again, starting with Genesis, and reading at least three or four chapters a day. Underline, meditate, jot down notes, and write down thoughts. Spend at least one month alone in the book of Psalms underscoring in your Bible the great promises of God. Join a Bible study and don't miss the sessions. You will find a supernatural power. Only the Bible, God's word, will bring you to grips with what has happened, and give the only logical, true explanation for it all. Only the Bible will bring the comfort, the challenge, and the vision for the future you must have.

STEP 3: DON'T HESITATE TO TALK ABOUT THE DECEASED!

Our culture has almost taught us that we need to forget, brush it all out of our minds and think about something else. Wrong! We never hesitated to talk about them while they were alive, we need to talk about them MORE now that they are gone from us. There is a therapy in verbalizing memories. Don't fear it, God's healing will be real sooner for you if you are willing to express your true feelings about him or her. A woman in our congregation was told just a week after her husband died, that she should immediately dispose of his belongings, sell the house they had lived in, the car he drove, the golf clubs he used, etc. She came to me to ask advice about the advice! I told her to do what seemed natural to her, and not try to sweep the precious memories under the rug. She took that advice, and her healing and deliverance from grief came much sooner than she or any of us expected.

STEP 4: PRAY THAT YOU WILL COOPERATE WITH GOD IN HIS REPLACEMENT PROGRAM

I believe the Lord has a way of replacing our loved ones, whether it's a spouse, a parent, a child, a brother or sister. Cooperate with God in it. You may be saying, "O, no one could possibly replace _____." In a sense, that's true, but in another sense, you will be surprised whom God will bring into your life to fill the void.

GOOD GRIEF! Yes, it really is good, though we may not think so at the moment. But, when it has run its course, and we have seen the strong arm of God in its midst, it is . . . GOOD GRIEF! Probably the best part of grief's goodness is that it drives us to God, because it is the one thing we can't handle alone. Whittier said it best, I think:

> When sorrow comes, as come it must,
> In God a man must put his trust.
> There is no power in mortal speech
> The anguish of his soul to reach,
> No voice, however sweet and low,
> Can comfort him or ease the blow.

> He cannot from his fellow men
> Take strength that will sustain him then.
> With all that kindly hands will do,
> And all that love may offer, too,
> He must believe throughout the test,
> That God has willed it for the best.

> We who would be his friends are dumb,
> Words from our lips but feebly come.
> We feel as we extend our hands,
> That One Power only understands
> And truly knows the reason why
> So beautiful a life must die.

GOOD GRIEF

We realize how helpless then
Are all the gifts of mortal men.
No words which we have power to say
Can take the sting of grief away—
That Power which marks the sparrow's fall
Must comfort and sustain us all.

When sorrow comes, as come it must,
In God a man must place his trust.
With all the wealth which he may own,
He cannot meet the test alone,
And only he may stand serene
Who has a faith on which to lean.

—*John Greenleaf Whittier*

WHERE ARE YOU GOING?

I remember visiting the Honolulu zoo. Visitors who pass through the feline section can't help but notice a bobcat in a squirrel cage running so fast they can't see his feet. The sign used to read: "This cat can run at speeds up to 45 miles per hour." But the ironic thing that everyone notices, is that the cat gets nowhere! Day in, day out, he runs and runs and runs . . . and gets nowhere! He never really leaves the place he commences, yet runs furiously! Sound familiar?

How long has it been since you asked yourself the question, "WHERE AM I GOING?" I'm not really talking about intermediate stops like work, the bank, the store, etc. Where are you headed in life? What is your objective in life? What is your final destination? The standing joke of airline pilots is the announcement that comes on and says: "GOOD AFTERNOON FOLKS, WE HAVE NO IDEA WHERE WE ARE GOING, BUT WE ARE MAKING EXCELLENT TIME!" What a description of much of our age.

Indecision keeps many from going places. History reveals that President Buchanan rode the fence when the nation was falling apart because it was politically expedient. The result was a civil war, because a president decided not to decide anything. A policy of drift only gathers barnacles. Ours has become an age of saying yes and no at the same time. Some have coined a new word, "YO." (That's yes and no put together.)

Rutted people are going nowhere. Many are in a rut. They do the same thing every Monday, go the same places every Tuesday, see the same people every Wednesday, drive the same route every Thursday, and wear the same suit every Friday. A sign on a terribly muddy road in the hills of East Tennessee read: "CHOOSE YOUR RUTS CAREFULLY, YOU'LL BE IN THEM FOR THE NEXT 5 MILES." How true, how true! Sometimes, it's providential when we are forced out of our ruts by God's circumstances. In the early 1970's when the aero-space industry fell flat, thousands of people on the west coast found themselves suddenly unemployed. One man, who had been an engineer for 25 years, when terminated from a large airline company, took the little bit of savings he had and opened a small donut shop. This is what you call a career change! His business boomed. He opened a second shop. Today he has a whole string of donut shops. He got out of a rut, albeit not by his own choosing. Are you in a rut, and keep driving over the same terrain daily, weekly, monthly, yearly? Maybe it's time for you to "break out" and venture for God.

The bumper sticker read: "WE OWE, WE OWE, SO IT'S OFF TO WORK WE GO." Humorous and clever, but probably painfully true. So many are in bondage to debt by easy to get credit, they will serve out the rest of their life sentence doing nothing but working to pay off the bills. Debt is but one rut, there are many, many more.

God never intended that His people be on the fence, aimlessly wandering, with no goal in sight. Of course, the major objective of every true believer is to glorify God with all we are and have. Paul said, "But one thing I do . . ." (Phil. 3:13). He also said, "I do not run aimlessly, I do not box as beating the air . . ." (I Cor. 9:26). Maybe the best place to start is for you to sit down and ask, "What do I want to accomplish for God before I die?" Be specific, not vague, don't deal in generalities. Don't answer that by saying, "To reach as many people for Christ as I can, wherever I can." It's best to say, "To reach 1000 people for Christ in Bombay, India, by the year 2000. (Or wherever and whenever.)

The truth is, however, you can go nowhere until you are free to go. Whether you are behind the bars of fear, lust, anger, bitterness, or whatever, you need to be free. Jesus once said, "If the Son makes you free, you will be free indeed" (John 8:36). Don't settle for the freedom the world offers. Freedom is not the right to do what I want, but the responsibility to do what I ought. Only Jesus Christ can bring that kind of freedom in your life. He who came to set the captives free stands ready to set YOU free.

The world's recipe for freedom reeks of bondage. It is a cheap escapism that leaves us deceived and deluded. Several years ago a New York bus driver became wearied of impatient passengers and demanding schedules. Not having "wings like a dove" with which to disappear, he simply let off his last passenger and drove his city bus 1500 miles south to Florida. Of course he was caught, and the last state became worse than the first. He found himself broke, in jail, and shameful of what he had done. Freedom doesn't come by escaping. That's not freedom, but a world of fantasy, and lasts but a short time.

Many people evade and avoid their responsibility to plan ahead, set goals, and get some order to their lives, because Jesus said, "Do not be anxious about tomorrow" (Matt. 6:34). Let me assure you Jesus did not say, "Do not even consider tomorrow." His teaching was not a suggestion that we not plan, anticipate, and make provision. His teaching is that we not get uptight about the future so that we begin fretting and sweating its outcome. If you fail to plan, you plan to fail. History is strewn with the wreckage of people who sought to hop-scotch through life with no destination in mind. Jesus made it clear, I think, that planning ahead is wise.

If you would really be free, there are some myths that need to be exploded. In their place, we need to establish firm principles that are unwavering.

FREEDOM PRINCIPLE #1 VICTORY AND FREEDOM COME BY SURRENDER, NOT STRUGGLE!

Our society teaches that if you want something, "Go for it!" Be aggressive, seize it, go for it! I am convinced that victory is never attained by struggle and hard work, but by surrender. Deliverance belongs to those who have learned that they can't deliver themselves. A drowning person is never rescued while he's thrashing, struggling and fighting in the water. It's when he gives up and surrenders himself over to his rescuers that he is saved. It's when the alcoholic realizes he can't extricate himself from his damning addiction, and that he must have power and help far beyond his own that he's on the road to recovery. Until that moment of truth, all other programs fail. So if you need God's deliverance in any area of your life, it begins with your surrender to Him.

FREEDOM PRINCIPLE #2 BELIEVE IN THE ABILITY OF GOD TO DELIVER

Shadrach, Meshach, and Abednego learned this. Their famous words before being put into the fiery furnace were:

. . . our God whom we serve is able to deliver us from the burning fiery furnace; and He will deliver us out of your hand, O King (Dan. 3:17).

What confidence! Their hair wasn't even singed. Their belief in God's ability took them through that ordeal, and indeed deliverance came. O, how we need to assert that kind of faith in God's ability. When you realize God really is able to do far more abundantly than all that we can ask or think, deliverance isn't too far behind. Theologians have argued for years whether or not God is still doing miracles today. But you know who doesn't argue about those miracles? Those who experience them! They experience them before anybody has taught them they aren't supposed to experience them! If we need a restoration of anything today it's faith in God's ability to do the impossible. If God can deliver the Israelites from Egyptian bondage captured by the stubbornness of Pharaoh, then He can deliver you from what binds you. He's waiting for your faith in His ability.

I'm always impressed with the story of the woman with the flow of blood (Mark 5). Jesus told her that it was her faith that made her well. Many "brushed" Jesus that day, but only one touched Him. Many talked with Him, but only one made a claim on His power. Jesus always honors those who trust His power by their simple faith. Deliverance belongs to those whose God is big enough for the impossible.

FREEDOM PRINCIPLE #3 YOUR COOPERATION WITH GOD IS INDISPENSIBLE!

Many have been lulled into thinking . . . "God does it all!" Of course, to be sure, God is the initiator and the provider of strength for us to respond, but while God opens the doors, WE must walk through them. God will never do for you what He has designed for you to do yourself. I could go to my car, with keys in my pocket, and sit in the driver's seat, with hands on the steering wheel and expect God to start the car. I don't think He ever would, because He had provided for me a set of keys, an ignition, and the physical stamina and mental capacity to insert one into the other and turn it on! On more than one occasion, Jesus said, "Rise, take up your pallet and walk." It was in the rising that often the healing came! Of course it came from the Lord, but the sick cooperated by obedience. God never promised us deliverance when we violate or ignore the laws He's already put into operation. And while His deliverance isn't limited to those laws, we have no license to ignore them.

FREEDOM PRINCIPLE #4 LEAVE THE TIMING TO GOD

We are part of the "instantaneous" age of "having it now." Fortunately, God doesn't work on our timetable. Beware of any and all who want to "demand" from a sovereign God something to be delivered according to their time perimeters. We must avoid the trap of the man who prayed, "Lord, give me patience, and I want it NOW!" There is something incongruous about our demanding and commanding God to do something for us, then setting the time limits in which He's to do it. "O," but some will say, "all His miracles in the Bible were instantaneous." First of all, they weren't. Secondly, if they were, who says God is obligated to do now exactly what He did then, the same way, in the same time frame? This does not dilute either His power to deliver nor His desire to free us. Often, what seems like His delay is our unwillingness to cooperate, or our unwillingness to wait.

Centuries ago God made an astounding promise to the young prophet, Jeremiah. Because scripture is alive and relevant to the here and now, that promise is really made to you. It goes like this:

> Be not afraid of them, for I am with you to deliver you, says the Lord (Jer. 1:8).

It is true, "DELIVERANCE BELONGS TO THE LORD" (Ps. 3:8). He stands ready to deliver you, here and now. He only awaits the expression of your desire. If He can deliver the dumb demoniac from madness, the blind from darkness, the deaf from muteness, the crippled from paralysis, and the dead from stillness, He can deliver you from whatever it is that binds you now.

Years ago, a western Oklahoma homesteader lived for 38 years on a wind-swept, dust-infested farm, eking out of life a bare existence of poverty. He tried to sell the farm, but was only offered $700 in the dust bowl days. One day when he was trying to decide what to do, an oil company representative came and asked if he might drill on his property. Permission granted, oil was found. In all, four gushers brought in- nearly $1000 per week. All those years that farmer had lived on top of black gold and lived in poverty. What a parable! So many today are enslaved to something, living in abject spiritual poverty and bondage, while beneath is God's great reservoir of wealth. Will you say with Daniel, ". . . our God whom we serve is able to deliver us . . ." (Dan. 3:17)? Deliverance belongs to the Lord, but it's for you. How about it?

So what is the "therefore" to it all? Just this . . . Jesus indeed came to set at liberty those who were captive. In Him we are freed from the guilt and damnation of sin, from eternal death, from hell, and in this life, certainly all that would keep us from total devotion to Him. Paul's sermon at Antioch has an astounding statement in it:

> Let it be known to you therefore, brethren, that through this man, forgiveness of sins is proclaimed to you, and by him everyone THAT BELIEVES IS FREED FROM EVERYTHING FROM WHICH YOU COULD NOT BE FREED BY THE LAW OF MOSES (Acts 13:38-39).

What an affirmation! It's true. We are "FREE AT LAST." Let's claim it, live it, and thank God for it! It is a free people that will make a bound world desire what we have in Christ.